VICTOR E. HOVEN

SHADOW
AND
SUBSTANCE

BY
VICTOR E. HOVEN, M.A., B.D., D.D.

Professor of Biblical Doctrine, Christian Evidences and
Hermeneutics, Northwest Christian College,
Eugene, Oregon; Author of *The Purpose
and Progress in Prophecy*

WIPF & STOCK · Eugene, Oregon

Wipf and Stock Publishers
199 W 8th Ave, Suite 3
Eugene, OR 97401

Shadow and Substance
By Hoven, Victor E.
ISBN 13: 978-1-5326-4592-1
Publication date 12/19/2017
Previously published by The Bethany Press, 1934

PREFACE

In speaking of the relation between the types of the Old Testament and the gospel they prefigured, Paul calls the former "a shadow" and the latter "the body," or substance (Col. 2:17). Having thus linked type and antitype, it follows that the gospel must have existed in the mind of Jehovah at the time he set the type. We reason that without reality there can be no shadow. In harmony with this thought, it is recorded that God chose us in Christ "before the foundation of the world" (Eph. 1:4).

The necessity of giving attention to typical teaching arises from the fact that the types "were written for our admonition" (1 Cor. 10:11). As a part of the Jewish Scriptures their design was to make us "wise unto salvation through faith which is in Christ Jesus" (2 Tim. 3:15). With that in mind this volume is intended to assist the reader in his effort to acquire knowledge of divine wisdom in order to enter into its enjoyment through practice. The material for these studies has been used by the author in the classroom for a number of years.

From the table of contents it will be noticed that the subject matter is not exhaustive. However, the aim is to consider the fundamental types in the great range of divine revelation so as to impart a fair understanding of this kind of teaching.

For the sake of clearness the method employed is the outline form concisely stated. The Bible is allowed to be its own interpreter without cramping it by human opinions. The abundance of references will enable the student to become acquainted with "the word of wisdom" and to speak "the language of Canaan."

THE AUTHOR.

INTRODUCTION

A. MAN'S NEED OF DIVINE INSTRUCTION—

1. *Sin separates.*—It is impossible for a holy God to fellowship sin (Isa. 59:2). Man's inherent need is God (Ps. 63:1). Therefore he wants to know where to find him and how to get back to him (Job 23:3).

2. *Revelation restores.*—In dealing with man's moral and spiritual bankruptcy, God's first act of recovery was information (Gen. 3:15). The purpose in divine revelation is to offer definite terms on which connection between God and man broken by sin may be restored. To that end the call to the sinner reads, "Incline your ear, and come unto me; hear, and your soul shall live" (Isa. 55:3; cp. John 5:25). From this it is clear that the process of man's salvation is not an effort to adjust God to man, but man to God.

B. GOD'S METHOD OF TEACHING—

1. *By words* (Psalm 32:8).—By words of the devil man was lost. He heard, believed and obeyed a lie (Gen. 3:16). By the word of God he is saved. He must hear, believe and obey the truth (Acts 11:13, 14).

2. *By life.*—The men of faith and obedience whose history is found in the Bible exemplify and enforce the verbal revelation. This is manifest in

Jesus (Matt. 11:29), in Paul (1 Tim. 1:16), in the lives of faith recorded in Hebrews 11, and in the church (2 Cor. 3:2).

3. *By types*—

a) Definition.—The word "type" comes from the Greek *typos,* the root meaning of which is a blow; also a mark, or impression left by a blow. The latter meaning is employed in the Scriptures. In John 20:25 it is a mark left by the nails. In Acts 7:43 it is used with reference to an image formed from an original design. In Acts 7:44 and Hebrews 8:5 it is a model of the real thing. In Romans 6:17 it is used to designate a mould, or imprint. In 1 Corinthians 10:6, 11 it is employed in relation to fleshly Israel as a type of the church. In Romans 5:14 its use is in analogy of one person to another. By these Scriptures we are led to the conclusion that the general meaning of the word "type," as used in the Bible, is the imprint of model of the original.

b) Usage.—The employment of the type in the divine economy was twofold.

1) To teach.—It was "a figure," a parable, or illustration "for the time present" (Heb. 9:9). As picture-lessons of divine truth, types were adapted to the spiritual childhood of the race, and are comparable to the method of teaching by means of pictures and objects in the primary grades of our public schools.

2) *To predict.*—Paul says of the tabernacle and its services that it was "a shadow of the good things to come" (Heb. 10:1). All types were dim pictures of redemption through the coming Messiah. They were so dark that neither angels nor men could get their full significance. Paul speaks of their time as "the dispensation of the mystery" which was finally "made known through the church" (Eph. 3:9-11). In this respect the divine type was like the printer's type. While smeared with the black ink, it does not appear to contain much information; but when the impression, or the antitype, is made, it becomes the intellectual light of the world. Likewise our spiritual light has come out of that which was once a dark mystery. When Jesus, the antitype, came, he said, "I am the light of the world" (John 8:12).

C. WHAT MAY BE CONSIDERED AS TYPES?—

1. *That which is so designated in the Scriptures.* —Adam is said to be "a figure of him that was to come" (Rom. 5:14). The law contained "a shadow of the good things to come" (Heb. 10:1). The Hebrew nation is used "by way of example" (1 Cor. 10:6, 11). There was to be a prophet like Moses (Deut. 18:18); a priest like Melchizedek (Ps. 110:4); a king like David (Isa. 9:6, 7). Noah's salvation through water was a type of Christian baptism (1 Pet. 3:20, 21). But the scriptural

designation of what is typical does not exhaust the subject. God has left some things for man to discover.

2. *That which contains transferred names.*—Christ is called David (Ezek. 34:24), our passover (1 Cor. 5:7), and the first fruits (1 Cor. 15:23). Since these terms have been transferred to Christ, it follows that the person and things they represent were intended as types of him. In the same way Jerusalem in Judea was typical of the heavenly Jerusalem (Heb. 12:22; Gal. 4:26). For the same reason circumcision under the Old Covenant typified the cutting away from the heart all things impure and unholy under the New Covenant (Rom. 2:28, 29).

3. *That which is analogous.*—It was not necessary for the writers to name every type, any more than it was necessary for Jesus to interpret every parable he spoke. From a few explanations of both classes the reader is left with the Scriptures and his own judgment to determine the rest.

Abraham was a type of faith and obedience, and of what a Christian's attitude should be toward the things of this world (Gen. 12:1-4; 13:7-9). Isaac was typical of the Messiah in the miraculous birth, divine name, and personal experience (Gen. 17:16-19; 22). In all probability Joseph was a type, for there are many things in his character and doings that are analogous to the character and work of Christ. The cities of refuge appointed for the manslayer (Num. 35:9-34) were typical of Christ to whom we may flee for refuge (Heb. 6:18-20). Though these are not spoken of as types, the analogy between them and New Testament facts is so evident that one cannot miss the intended teaching.

D. TYPES IN RELATION TO REVELATION—

1. *The divine plan in revelation.*—One characteristic of the Bible is its progressive revelation. To the observing student there is evidence of a gradual and successive unfolding of Jehovah's plan of saving man from sin. From Adam to Christ there is a marked organic unity which culminates in Christianity. The divine plan develops along three distinct lines: history, type, and prophecy. In each of these there is revelation of the divine purpose. In the history of the chosen people we are made to see how Jehovah used human agency and natural means. In type and prophecy, revelation is the result of a mental miracle performed by the Spirit of God. Finally it is discovered that all three lines focalize in the Messiah who answers to the purpose in human history, the predictions of the prophets and fills out in clear details the dimly outlined picture of the type.

2. *The necessity of a gradual revelation.*—The reason for a progressive revelation is found in man's mental and spiritual condition after the fall. The divine image in him was greatly marred

by sin, and instruction must be adapted to his condition. In the whole compass of sacred history we find only three dispensations of religion. They are the Patriarchal, or family; the Mosaic, or national; the Christian, or world wide.

Of these, the first two only demand our attention at present. In the Patriarchal Age we have that which exactly answers to infancy. The awful consequences of sin had not yet dawned upon the human mind. The patriarchs walked with God in the beauty and simplicity of childlike faith before the age of accountability. In this age the principal type of teaching was in connection with the altar. In the Mosaic Age man was dealt with differently. He was placed under law, which indicates that he had arrived at the age of accountability. In spiritual perception he had passed from infancy to childhood. This fact is illustrated and applied in Galatians 4:1-7 to show that Christians are not under the law of Moses. In this period all the Old Testament types are completed. To the altar of the Patriarchal Age a great deal of new material is added, hence there is a distinct advance in type teaching. The whole is centered in the tabernacle worship, which summarizes in type all the facts of Christianity.

CONTENTS

	PAGE
INTRODUCTION	v

A. Man's need of divine instruction.
  1. *Sin separates.*
  2. *Revelation restores.*
B. God's method of teaching.
  1. *By words.*
  2. *By life.*
  3. *By types.*
     a) Definition.
     b) Usage.
        1) To teach.
        2) To predict.
C. What may be considered as types?
  1. *That which is so designated in the Scriptures.*
  2. *That which contains transferred names.*
  3. *That which is analogous.*
D. Types in relation to revelation.
  1. *The divine plan in revelation.*
  2. *The necessity of a gradual revelation.*

I. ADAM — 1
  1. *Origin.*
  2. *Constitution.*
  3. *Dominion.*
  4. *Wedlock.*
  5. *Character.*
     a) Original perfection.
     b) Disobedience.
  6. *Accomplishment.*
     a) Giver of human life through generation.
     b) Brought sin into the world.
     c) Brought death into the world.
     d) Made sinners.

II. THE GARDEN OF EDEN — 9
  1. *A dwelling place or home.*
  2. *Its river.*
  3. *The tree of life.*

xi

II. THE GARDEN OF EDEN—Cont'd

4. *The presence of God.*
5. *Employment.*
6. *Man glorified.*
7. *The curse.*

III. SACRIFICE — 14

1. *Origin.*
2. *Essentials.*
   a) The altar.
   b) The sacrifice.
   c) The priest.
      1) To mediate.
      2) To sacrifice.
      3) To sympathize.

IV. THE FLOOD — 20

1. *Proclamation.*
2. *Faith.*
3. *Obedience.*
4. *Through water.*
5. *Unity.*
6. *Covenant.*

V. ABRAHAM — 25

1. *His call.*
   a) Divine and verbal.
   b) To leave the old life and begin a new.
   c) To fame and fortune.
2. *His faith.*
   a) The basis of his faith.
   b) The strength of his faith.
3. *His obedience.*
4. *His attitude toward the things of this world.*

VI. ISAAC — 32

1. *Miraculous birth.*
2. *Divinely named.*
3. *Persecuted.*
4. *Sacrificed.*

CONTENTS XIII

PAGE
VII. MELCHIZEDEK _ _ _ _ _ _ _ _ _ 37
    1. "Priest of God Most High."
    2. "King of righteousness."
    3. "King of Salem."
    4. "Without father, without mother."
    5. "Without genealogy."
    6. "Having neither beginning of days nor end of life."
    7. "Consider how great this man was."

VIII. JOSEPH _ _ _ _ _ _ _ _ _ _ _ 44
    1. *His humiliation.*
        a) Hated by his brethren.
        b) Sold for the price of a slave.
        c) Tempted and tried.
    2. *His exaltation.*
        a) Providential events which led to his exaltation.
        b) His power on the throne.
    3. *The divine purpose.*
        a) To exalt one whom men had rejected.
        b) To produce in those who rejected him a sense of their guilt.
        c) To preserve life.
        d) To render service without cost.

IX. ISRAEL _ _ _ _ _ _ _ _ _ _ _ _ 52
    1. *The unredeemed.*
    2. *The redeemer.*
    3. *The redemption.*
    4. *The holy nation.*
    5. *The pilgrimage.*
    6. *The Jordan.*
    7. *Canaan.*

X. MOSES _ _ _ _ _ _ _ _ _ _ _ _ 60
    1. *Providentially preserved.*
    2. *Sent as a deliverer.*
    3. *Officiated as lawgiver.*
    4. *Worked as builder.*
    5. *Served as ruler and intercessor.*
    6. *Was a distinguished prophet.*

CONTENTS

	PAGE
XI. AARON	68

1. *Induction into office.*
    a) The call.
    b) Publicity.
    c) Washing.
    d) Anointing.
    e) Consecration.
    f) Entry into office.
2. *Dress.*
    a) The white garments.
        1) The breeches.
        2) The coat.
        3) The girdle.
        4) The mitre.
    b) The colored garments.
        1) The breastplate.
        2) The ephod.
        3) The robe of the ephod.
3. *Duties.*
    a) To offer sacrifice for sin.
    b) To apply the blood.
    c) To bless the people.

XII. DAVID	76

1. *Born in Bethlehem.*
2. *Of the royal tribe of Judah.*
3. *Divinely chosen and anointed.*
4. *Manifested to Israel.*
5. *Tested and approved.*
6. *A reign of righteousness and mercy.*
7. *An invincible warrior.*

XIII. GIFTS AND SACRIFICES	83

1. *The burnt offering.*
    a) The victim.
        1) Within reach of all.
        2) A male without blemish.
        3) Divinely selected.
    b) Disposal of the victim.
        1) By the offerer.
        2) By the priest.
    c) The design.

2. *The meal offering.*
   a) The substance offered.
      1) Grain.
      2) Oil.
      3) Frankincense.
      4) No leaven or honey.
      5) Salt.
   b) Disposal of the offering.
      1) Jehovah's part.
      2) The priest's part.
3. *The peace offering.*
   a) The victim.
   b) The sacrificial acts.
      1) By the offerer.
      2) By the priest.
   c) The consumption of the offering.
      1) The victim was shared.
      2) The meat was eaten while fresh.
      3) The meat was eaten in purity.
   d) The time of the offering.
4. *The sin and trespass offerings.*
   a) The sin offering.
      1) The kind of sins treated.
      2) Gradation of sacrifice according to responsibility.
      3) The victim without the camp.
   b) The trespass offering.
      1) The kind of wrongs involved.
         (a) In things of Jehovah.
         (b) In things of one's neighbor.
      2) The legal requirements.
         (a) Confession.
         (b) Restitution.
         (c) Atonement.
   c) Requirements of a sinner in the church.
      1) Repentance.
      2) Prayer.
      3) Confession.
      4) Restoration.
   d) The atoning blood.

CONTENTS

	PAGE
XIV. AARON'S SONS	107

1. *They were divinely called.*
2. *They answered the call.*
3. *They were set apart according to divine directions.*
   a) Publicity.
   b) Washing.
   c) Vestments.
   d) Sacrifices.
   e) Sanctification.
   f) Days of consecration.

XV. OBJECTIVE TEACHING ON SIN AND HOLINESS — 115

1. *Clean and unclean animals.*
   a) To separate Jehovah's people.
   b) To teach holiness.
   c) To give a picture of the character of sin.
      1) Sin is unclean and to be avoided.
      2) Sin is brutish.
      3) Sin brings destruction.
2. *Purification at child birth.*
   a) Sin in relation to birth.
      1) Sin and our original parents.
      2) The propagation of sin.
   b) Sin as an unclean thing.
      1) Separation of the mother.
      2) Circumcision of the male child.
   c) The means for cleansing.
3. *Leprosy.*
   a) Leprosy of person.
      1) The symptoms.
      2) The characteristics.
         (a) It is transmissible.
         (b) It spreads gradually.
         (c) It is exceedingly loathsome.
         (d) It makes one insensible.
         (e) It separates.
         (f) It is incurable by earthly means.

3) The cleansing.
   (a) The first cleansing.
      (1) The priest goes forth to meet him.
      (2) The process of cleansing.
   (b) The second cleansing.
      (1) The several offerings.
      (2) Provision for the poor.
  b) Leprosy of garments.
   1) The signs of infection.
   2) The method of procedure.
      (a) All the people on watch.
      (b) Inspection by the priest.
      (c) Treatment of garments.
         (1) "Burn."
         (2) "Wash."
  c) Leprosy of houses.
   1) The treatment of the plague.
   2) The atonement for the house.

XVI. HOLY SEASONS _ _ _ _ _ _ _ _ _ _ 136

1. *The Sabbath.*
   a) Observance.
      1) In the home.
      2) In the sanctuary.
   b) Design.
      1) It was a day of rest, worship, and rejoicing.
      2) It was commemorative.
         (a) Of the creation.
         (b) Of Israel's bondage in Egypt and deliverance.
      3) It was a sign between Jehovah and Israel.
   c) Type.
      1) Of rest in Christ here.
      2) Of rest through Christ hereafter.
2. *The Passover.*
   a) The time.
   b) The victim.
      1) It was without blemish.
      2) It was to be a mature male.
      3) It was killed at even on the fourteenth.

XVI. HOLY SEASONS—Cont'd

        4) Its blood was sprinkled on the lintel and the two side-posts of the door.
        5) It was roasted whole, not a bone was broken.
        6) Its remains which were not eaten were burned.
    c) The eating.
        1) They were to eat it that night.
        2) They were to eat it as ready for the journey.
        3) They were to eat it in haste.
        4) They were to eat it without leaven.
        5) They were to eat it with bitter herbs.
        6) They were to eat it as a memorial.
  b) The feast of unleavened bread.
  e) The sheaf of the first fruits.

3. *The Feast of Weeks.*
  a) The observance of the day.
  b) The typical teaching.
    1) The significance of time.
    2) The meaning of offerings.

4. *The Feast of Trumpets.*
  a) The observance of the type.
  b) The teaching of the antitype.

5. *The Day of Atonement.*
  a) The order of services.
  b) The typical significance.
    1) The time.
    2) The high priest.
      (*a*) His dress.
      (*b*) His labors.
    3) The atonement.
      (*a*) Inability of the type.
      (*b*) The victims.
      (*c*) Necessity of blood.
      (*d*) Entering the Most Holy Place.
      (*e*) The live goat.

6. *The Feast of Tabernacles.*
  a) Characteristics of the feast.
    1) Its joyous activities.
    2) The dwelling in booths.
    3) The sacrifices.

  b) The type in fulfillment.
   1) The tent life.
   2) The rejoicing.

XVII. THE TABERNACLE _ _ _ _ _ _ _ 158
 1. *Names.*
  a) The "tent."
  b) "The tent of meeting."
  c) "The tabernacle of the testimony."
  d) "The house of Jehovah."
  e) "A sanctuary."
  f) "The temple of Jehovah."
 2. *History.*
  a) The date.
  b) The model.
  c) The material.
  d) The workmen.
  e) The cloud.
  f) The location.
 3. *Structure.*
  a) The court.
   1) Area.
   2) Contents.
    (*a*) The altar.
    (*b*) The laver.
  b) The sanctuary.
   1) Walls.
    (*a*) Boards.
    (*b*) Bars.
    (*c*) Foundation.
   2) Roof.
   3) The Holy Place.
    (*a*) Door.
    (*b*) Furniture.
     (1) The table of showbread.
     (2) The lampstand.
     (3) The altar of incense.
   4) The Most Holy Place.
    (*a*) The veil.
    (*b*) The ark.

CONCLUSIONS _ _ _ _ _ _ _ _ _ _ _ 181

I

ADAM

In Romans 5:12-17 we are told that Adam "is a figure [type] of him that was to come," that is, of Christ. The apostle parallels the two characters in order to show that the ruin brought by the one is canceled by the other. In addition to this remarkable passage, other portions of the divine revelation are necessary to a fuller understanding of type and antitype. It will be observed that in some particulars the two heads of humanity are alike, while in others they are opposite.

1. *Origin.*—The preamble to the creation of Adam reads, "Let us make man in our image, after our likeness" (Gen. 1:26). The fact of his creation is made known in the words, "And Jehovah God formed man of the dust of the ground, and breathed into his nostrils the breath of life; and man became a living soul" (Gen. 2:7). "The Spirit of God" was the agent Jehovah employed in forming the body of Adam (Job 33:4). Because he came into being without human parents, he is called "the son of God" (Luke 3:38).

Christ, called by Paul "the last Adam" (1 Cor. 15:45), came into this world without a human father but with a human mother. As with the first Adam, so God prepared the body of Jesus by the Holy Spirit (Heb. 10:5; Luke 1:35). The latter fact is no more incredible than the former. In each case a miracle was necessary and God was able to perform it (Matt. 19:26). Because the body of Jesus was supernaturally formed, he is called "the son of God."

2. *Constitution.*—Adam first was made in the image and after the likeness of his creator. That elevated him above the animal creation and placed him "but little lower than God" (Ps. 8:5). Not that in body he was like his maker, for "God is a Spirit" (John 4:24), but in spiritual attributes he was crowned with glory and honor. That is the eternal difference between him and all other creatures, and it constituted him the first perfect representative of God on earth.

Christ, "the second man is of heaven" (1 Cor. 15:47). Physically he became like his type in that he came to this world in a human body, but spiritually he was superior. Adam was "the image of God"; Christ was "the very image" of God (Heb. 1:3). For that reason John, in speaking of the pre-existence and office of Jesus, declares "the Word was God" (John 1:1). Hence Paul could say "God was in Christ" (2 Cor. 5:19). Thus in constitution he was divine as well as human, and he stands before us as the last and most perfect representative of God on this earth.

3. *Dominion.*—God said to Adam, "have dominion" over the earth, the sea and all living things (Gen. 1:26, 28, 29; Ps. 8:5-8). He was given au-

thority to govern and use the whole mundane creation. This seems to be honor and glory enough for any man. Because Adam introduced sin and on account of subsequent mismanagement, this whole estate is doomed to bankruptcy, which necessitates "new heavens and a new earth, wherein dwelleth righteousness" (2 Pet. 3:13).

Christ, having finished his work on earth, went back to heaven "to receive for himself a kingdom, and to return" (Luke 19:12). His domain is the universe (Matt. 28:18; Acts 2:36; 1 Pet. 3:22). The Father "put all things in subjection under his feet," God excepted (1 Cor. 15:27). With honor and glory he was crowned "because of the suffering of death" (Heb. 2:9). His management is far superior to that of the first Adam, so that "his kingdom is an everlasting kingdom, and all dominions shall serve and obey him" (Dan. 7:27).

4. *Wedlock.*—Adam was created a social being. On that account Jehovah said, "It is not good that the man should be alone; I will make him a help meet for him" (Gen. 2:18). Accordingly, he put him to sleep, removed a rib from his side and from it created a woman whom he presented to the man to be his companion for life (Gen. 2:21-24).

This union of Adam and his wife is analogous to Christ and his church. At his crucifixion his side was opened with a spear. The blood which flowed from the open wound became the means by which the church was created, for that blood "cleanseth us from all sin" (1 John 1:7). On account of this fact the church is spoken of as the spouse of Christ. Paul wrote to the Corinthians, "I espoused you to one husband, that I might present you as a pure virgin to Christ" (2 Cor. 11:2). In his letter to the Ephesians he compares husband and wife to Christ and the church. As the husband is head of the wife, so Christ is head of the church. The husband is to love the wife, "even as Christ also loved the church, and gave himself up for it" (Eph. 5:22-25).

5. *Character*—

a) Original perfection.—This is a fact of divine revelation. As a part of creation, Adam "was very good" (Gen. 1:31). Solomon could say, "God made man upright" (Eccl. 7:29). In the beginning he was without sin and walked with God in the beauty of holiness.

The perfect character of Christ is also a matter of revelation. As a child, he "advanced in wisdom and stature, and in favor with God and men" (Luke 2:52). As an adult, he challenged the people of his day, and ours, in the words, "Which of you convicteth me of sin?" (John 8:46.) The declaration of the inspired writer is, he was "holy, guileless, undefiled, separated from sinners" (Heb. 7:26).

b) Disobedience.—This is the sad part of the story. Adam was tempted and yielded (Gen. 3:1-

6). This converted him into a rebel against divine authority, occasioned the Bible to be written, and the Messiah to be sent.

In contrast with Adam, Christ was obedient. When he volunteered his mission and service to the Father, he said: "Lo, I am come (In the roll of the the book it is written of me) To do thy will, O God" (Heb. 10:7). This purpose he triumphantly supported to the end of his earthly career. In all things his Father's will was his will (John 4:34). He too was tempted by the devil, but yielded not (Matt. 4:1-11).

6. *Accomplishment*—

a) Giver of human life through generation.— "The first man is of the earth," and "As is the earthy, such are they also that are earthy" (1 Cor. 15:47, 48). His posterity inherit from him their earthly body. Because of this fact, Paul could say to the Athenians, God "made of one every nation of men" (Acts 17:26). In the sacred writings Adam is honored as the fountainhead of the whole human race.

Christ is the giver of spiritual life through regeneration. In contrast with the type, he "is of heaven, and as is the heavenly, such are they also that are heavenly" (1 Cor. 15:47, 48). He gives to men "the right to become children of God" through rebirth (John 1:12, 13; 3:5). In that process they "become partakers of the divine nature" (2 Pet. 1:4), take on the Lord's image and are declared heirs of life eternal. In this matter God has honored Christ as the spiritual head of all who receive him (Eph. 1:22, 23).

b) Brought sin into the world.—"Through one man sin entered into the world" (Rom. 5:12). "Sin is lawlessness" (1 John 3:4). Therefore the origin of sin on this earth was due to transgression of divine law by the first man. Here is the true account of the origin of evil, a subject which in the light of human reason alone has baffled all the philosophers and wise men of antiquity and modern times.

Christ cancels sin by his blood. He "poured it out for many unto remission of sins" (Matt. 26:28). It follows that God will not forgive anybody who does not avail himself of the blood of Christ. On the other hand, those who submit to its cleansing power can "glory in the cross" (Gal. 6:14) because there is no longer anything between them and God.

c) Brought death into the world, "death through sin" (Rom. 5:12).—This penalty for breaking God's law was enforced "in the day" of the crime (Gen. 2:17). Then spiritual death ensued through separation from God and physical death began its work on account of separation from the tree of life (Gen. 3:22). From that time to the present the words in Genesis 5, "and he died," have been the refrain of human history.

Christ conquered death by his resurrection. In his contrast of Adam and Christ, Paul points out that "by the trespass of the one the many died," but "the gift by the grace" of the other results in "justification," or acquittal from the sentence of death (Rom. 5:15, 16). Again Paul takes up the contrast of type and antitype in 1 Corinthians 15:21, 22, and positively declares that "as in Adam all die, so in Christ shall all be made alive." Because he will ransom his people from the power of the grave, the apostle could shout defiance to death (1 Cor. 15:55-57).

d) Made sinners.—"Through the one man's disobedience the many were made [constituted] sinners" (Rom. 5:19). One constitutional characteristic which all of Adam's descendants have inherited from him is a tendency to sin, and they do sin. That gives meaning to Genesis 5:3, "He begat a son in his own likeness, after his image" subsequent to the fall.

Christ makes many righteous. Continuing the parallel, the apostle says, "Through the obedience of the one shall the many be made [constituted] righteous." On account of the death of Christ, the sinner can become a "new man," that after God hath been created in righteousness and holiness of truth" (Eph. 4:24). As he received from Adam a tendency to sin, so in conversion Christ begets in him a desire to do righteousness (1 John 2:29).

From that moment his life is expressed in the words, "To me to live is Christ" (Phil. 1:21).

This type deals with the two most eminent personages that ever have lived upon this earth. Both entered this world in such manner as to make them distinct from all other men. Neither Adam nor Christ is to be considered as a private individual, but as a public person in relation to whom all mankind must be viewed. What each possessed, that he imparted to humanity. Therefore upon their character and conduct is suspended the destiny of the world.

II

THE GARDEN OF EDEN

In Revelation, the book of endings, is found the imagery of Genesis, the book of beginnings. The names of things connected with the first chapters of human history are transferred to the objects described in the last chapters of the book of human destiny. In both accounts is pictured the Paradise of God, the water of life and the tree of life (see Gen. 2; Rev. 2:7; 22:1, 2). This transfer of names leads to the conclusion that the Garden of Eden, the original dwelling place of human innocence, was intended as a type of heaven, the eternal dwelling place of human innocence restored.

1. *A dwelling place or home* (Gen. 2:8).—Eden is called in the Greek translation "Paradise," a Persian word for any garden of delight. Jehovah God planted it, hence it was a divinely prepared place. In it the Creator "put the man whom he had formed." God started him on a farm, not in a city.

The New Jerusalem is pictured as the saints' eternal home. Here they are addressed as "sojourners" and "pilgrims," but there they will move and travel no more. In John 14:2, 3 Jesus speaks of it as "my Father's house" whither he would go and prepare for his people "abiding-places "(marg.), i.e., places of permanent abode. As Eden of the type was prepared for those created in God's image, so heaven is prepared for those only who have been re-created after the divine image (Col. 3:10; Eph. 4:24; Rev. 21:27).

2. *Its river* (Gen. 2:10).—It sustained animal and vegetable life, hence it may be called "the river of life."

The New Jerusalem will also have its river of life (Rev. 22:1). Of old the Psalmist sang of this river (Ps. 46:4). This symbolism means that there will be divine support of spiritual life. As Christ is our life here (John 6:35), so he will continue to be the same there (Rev. 7:16, 17).

3. *The tree of life* (Gen. 2:9).—This tree seems to have been the medium through which life was transmitted from God to Adam and Eve. Its fruit kept them from sickness, old age and death (Gen. 3:22). It was designed to maintain in man "the power of an endless life."

In the Paradise of God will also be the tree of life (Rev. 22:2). The thought conveyed by the name of this tree is that the inhabitants of that better world shall never grow old, neither shall they experience illness, for the leaves of the tree are "for the healing of the nations"; "and death shall be no more" (Rev. 21:4). It will fulfill the promise of eternal life "to them that by patience in well-doing seek for glory and honor and incorruption" (Rom. 2:7).

4. *The presence of God* (Gen. 2:15-22).—In the beginning man had constant fellowship with his maker, who was his benefactor, preserver, teacher and object of worship. Jehovah taught Adam about his origin, constitution, and the things in the heavens and upon the earth. As a student he became so proficient that God had him name the beasts of the field and the birds of the heaven, a thing he could not have done if he had not known their characteristics, for upon these are based the names of the animal creation. We may conclude that Adam was the wisest man that has ever lived upon this earth, except Jesus Christ.

That man redeemed and glorified shall enjoy the presence of God, adore him and enjoy his personal instruction is a matter of certainty (Rev. 21:3; 22:4). Now Jehovah teaches man through nature and revelation, but then face to face. Man's capacity for knowledge is as endless as his spirit. What wealth of knowledge will an eternity with God bring! Moreover, adoration of God shall not be lacking (Rev. 15:2-4).

5. *Employment* (Gen. 2:15).—Work is one characteristic of personality. We were created thus, and in order to enjoy life to the full, employment is necessary. In this respect we are like our Maker, for he works (John 5:17).

Since work is one characteristic of our being, we may expect employment in heaven. That such our life will be there is definitely stated, "And his servants shall serve him" (Rev. 22:3). Just what that service will be is not revealed, but it will be divinely planned and directed.

6. *Man glorified.*—Adam and Eve were clothed with divine glory until that garment was removed by sin, for then "they knew that they were naked" (Gen. 3:7; cp. 1:26, 27). If sin did not affect this heavenly garment, why did they not discover before their disobedience that they were naked? If sin had not come to this world, there would be no need for tailors.

In the eternal life this glory-garment, lost by sin, will be restored to man (Phil. 3:20, 21). It was exhibited beforehand by our Savior on the Mount of Transfiguration (Matt. 17:2) and he promise is that "we shall be like him" (1 John 3:2).

7. *The curse* (Gen. 3:1-6, 14-19).—Into the glories of the first Paradise, sin entered and the curse was the result. In this situation man and earth have been laboring and sighing for six thousand years. To man the penalty of sin brought the experience of mental anguish, bodily suffering and severe toil. The whole creation below man "groaneth and travaileth in pain" (Rom. 8:20-22). Nothing in the whole universe escaped the effect of sin, hence the necessity for "new heavens and a new earth."

In the heavenly Paradise "there shall be no curse any more" (Rev. 22:3). The relief from sin and its effect will be eternal. Reasons for this condition are revealed. The tempter will be imprisoned forever (Rev. 20:10). Man redeemed, having been tested and approved through temptation, pain and suffering (James 1:12), will not repeat the mistake of the first man. Moreover, his new body will be free from the tendency to sin (1 Cor. 15:53). The announcement John heard from the throne was, "I make all things new" (Rev. 21:4, 5).

We have seen how the Garden of Eden was adapted to man's primitive constitution. Physically, it supplied all his needs; mentally, there was provision for his instruction under the Creator himself; spiritually, he was in fellowship with God. But in an unfortunate hour he lost all these privileges and plunged himself into despair. However, in God's revelation the curtain is lifted, and the eye of faith is permitted to behold Paradise regained through cleansing "in the blood of the Lamb" (Rev. 22:14; 7:14).

III

SACRIFICE

The first recorded sacrifice is found in Genesis 4:3-5 and it introduces the idea that there is something wrong between God and man. Since Jehovah accepted Abel's animal sacrifice and rejected Cain's vegetable offering, it is obvious that blood alone can make atonement and secure reconciliation.

All Old Testament sacrifices were typical of Christ. As a sacrifice, he is declared to have been "foreknown before the foundation of the world" (1 Pet. 1:20). It is his blood that "cleanseth us from all sin" (1 John 1:7). In him are found all the essentials of sacrifice. He is the altar, the sacrifice, the priest. He himself said, "I lay down my life" (John 10:15). Paul tells us, "We have an altar . . . Jesus" (Heb. 13:10, 12).

1. *Origin.*—Was sacrifice from heaven, or from men? This is unnecessarily a mooted question. Since sacrifice is a Bible subject, that book alone must be allowed to settle the controversy. It tells us that "by faith Abel offered unto God a more excellent sacrifice than Cain" (Heb. 11:4). It also informs us that faith rests upon divine testimony (Rom. 10:17). The conclusion is that Jehovah told Adam, Abel and Cain what and how to sacrifice. This is further evident from the fact,

"Jehovah had respect unto Abel and to his offering: but unto Cain and to his offering he had not respect." The divine approval and disapproval can be understood only in the light of previous instruction.

From the distinction of clean and unclean animals it is further argued that sacrifice was of divine origin. This distinction is first mentioned in Genesis 7:2. After the flood Noah "took of every clean beast, and of every clean bird, and offered burnt-offerings" unto Jehovah (Gen. 8:20). According to the Mosaic law only the clean animals were for sacrifice (Lev. 1:2, 10, 14).

The divine origin of sacrifice is confirmed by sound reason. It is not reasonable that the offender should dictate to the offended what shall be done to be cleared of guilt. The state does not proceed thus with the criminal, and it is unthinkable that God would do so with the transgressor of his law.

As Jehovah was the originator of the type, so to him the Scriptures trace the antitype. Christ is "the Lamb of God" (John 1:29). To make possible the sacrifice, Jehovah prepared for him a body (Heb. 10:5) which was finally nailed to the tree. In him is the ultimate explanation of the long line of priests, smoking altars and bleeding victims.

2. *Essentials.*—Of these there are three:

a) The altar.—Why have one? It "sanctifieth the gift" (Matt. 23:19) or sets it apart for a holy use. It is also the meeting place of God and man (Exod. 20:24).

Christ, our altar, was a sanctified man. Him "the Father sanctified and sent into the world" (John 10:36). He also sanctified, or set apart, his own life for a holy service which in all things manifested the will and pleasure of him that sent him (John 4:34; 8:29).

b) The sacrifice.—This was for atonement. Jehovah said, "The life of the flesh is in the blood; and I have given it to you upon the altar to make atonement for your souls" (Lev. 17:11). The principle involved is that *life lost is regained by life given*. In sacrifice the offerer witnessed two facts of eternal consequence: First, the death of the victim manifested the penalty of sin which is death (cp. Gen. 2:17); second, the shed blood offered him life, because animal life is in the blood. In order to present these two ideas, the slaying of an animal was the most perfect type conceivable.

The facts in the type furnish reasons for the Savior's crucifixion. In his death he was both a substitute for the sinner and a giver of life. Paul says, "We thus judge, that one died for all, therefore all died" (2 Cor. 5:14). His death therefore satisfied the law of God which, when broken, demands a victim. His shed blood, which contained his physical life, secures for man remission of sins (Matt. 26:28) and life eternal (Col. 2:13). Thus his blood is for atonement; and in his sacrificial death is seen the fundamental principle of all sacrifice, namely, life lost is regained by life given.

c) The priest.—According to Hebrews 5:1-3, his official ministry was:

1) To mediate.—He is "appointed for men in things pertaining to God." The work of a mediator was to restore peace and friendship between parties; or to mediate and confirm a covenant. In the Patriarchal Age the father of the family was the divinely appointed priest, or mediator. In the Mosaic Age priests, selected from the tribe of Levi, represented the Jewish nation before Jehovah.

Christ is the "one mediator between God and men" (1 Tim. 2:5). He interposed by his death and restored the peace and harmony between God and man broken by sin (Rom. 5:1). He made and confirmed the new covenant, the terms of which will secure salvation for lost humanity (Heb. 8:6; Luke 22:20). The divine arrangement is that we shall "draw near unto God through him" (Heb. 7:25).

2) To sacrifice.—According to divine appointment, the typical priest should "offer both gifts and sacrifices for sins." In the Patriarchal and Mosaic Dispensations he was the only person on earth who could treat sin, and he did it only by means of blood. The sacrifices he offered were the basis of his mediation between Jehovah and

the people. The altar served as the approach to God when there was blood upon it.

Like unto the type, but much greater, Christ is the only person now in the universe who can handle the matter of sin. Jehovah said of him, "Thou art a priest for ever after the order of Melchizedek" (Heb. 5:6). His offering is final: "There remaineth no more a sacrifice for sins" (Heb. 10:26). His shed blood is the basis of his mediation "before the face of God for us" (Heb. 9:24). Through his death we "were bought with a price" (1 Cor. 6:20) and when we go wrong, his plea before God is that he may spare the property of his Son.

3) To sympathize.—One qualification of the priest was that he should be able to "bear gently with the ignorant and erring." All men are oppressed by a great amount of trouble and woe, and one of their needs is sympathy. For that reason Jehovah said, "Comfort ye, comfort ye my people" (Isa. 40:1). In order to meet this need, it was necessary for the priest to live among the people and experience their life.

On this point our High Priest is fully qualified. "In the days of his flesh" he "learned obedience by the things which he suffered," hence "we have not a high priest that cannot be touched with the feeling of our infirmities; but one that hath been in all points tempted like as we are, yet without sin. Let us therefore draw near" (Heb. 5:7, 8;

4:15, 16). When he could no longer be here in person, he sent the Holy Spirit to be the comforter of the church (John 14:16, 17; Acts 9:31).

In the institution of sacrifice we see God and man coming together according to divine arrangement. It is the foundation of all revealed religion. Its redemptive character is seen in that man has lost life, and it is bought back by means of life which is in the blood. This important fact is first illustrated in type and finally made good in Christ who, by the sacrifice of himself, procured for us "eternal life" (1 John 5:11, 12).

IV

THE FLOOD

According to Genesis 6-8 and 1 Peter 3:20, 21, the immediate and remote purpose of this type was salvation. Because corruption and violence filled the earth, "God said unto Noah, The end of all flesh is come before me; but I will establish my covenant with thee." The apostle Peter, in referring to the salvation of Noah and his family, says that those "eight souls were saved through water: which also after a true likeness doth now save you, even baptism" (1 Pet. 3:20, 21). Careful attention to type and antitype will result in knowledge of God's requirements for salvation from sin and enjoyment of what he offers.

1. *Proclamation.*—God drew the pattern for the ark, gave it to Noah, told him to build accordingly and revealed to him its purpose. Not only did Jehovah proclaim these matters to Noah, but at the same time Noah himself was "a preacher of righteousness" (2 Pet. 2:5). It was a time of preaching.

As in the days of Noah, so now salvation is accomplished by preaching (Mark 16:15). According to Paul, the necessity for preaching is found in man's ignorance of God's plan of salvation (1 Cor. 1:21). Just as it was impossible for Noah by his own wisdom to know what he must do to save himself, his family and some of the animal creation, so it is beyond man's ability to devise what to do to be saved from sin.

2. *Faith.*—"By faith Noah ... prepared an ark" (Heb. 11:7). Since faith is the belief of testimony, the patriarch did not doubt a single word Jehovah had spoken to him concerning the impending judgment on sin and the means of escape. On the one hand, his faith prepared him to do something; on the other hand, it "condemned" the unbelieving antediluvian world.

One requirement unto salvation through Christ is faith in him (Acts 16:31). This faith is preparatory to action, hence the three thousand on Pentecost, after having heard Peter speak, asked, "What shall we do?" (Acts 2:37). Faith in the words of Jesus led Saul of Tarsus to say, "What shall I do, Lord?" (Acts 22:10). And as in the case of Noah, so now every person who believes the gospel with the intent of obeying it becomes a positive testimony against all unbelievers (cp. Matt. 12:41, 42).

3. *Obedience.*—In regard to constructing the ark, putting into it the animals specified, and entering into it with his family, we read: "Thus did Noah; according to all that God commanded him, so did he." That is one remarkable feature of this story. Not one word of argument or remonstrance was spoken by Noah; nor did he make any attempt, by

suggestion or otherwise, to modify the divine plan for his salvation.

Agreeable to the type, salvation from sin is conditioned on obedience to the commands of Christ. Thus it was with all who became Christians in the first century (see Acts 2:38; 3:19; 6:7; 22:16). That should be notable reading in our day of humanly modified divine law, and in many cases of totally ignoring the commands of the Savior.

4. *Through water.*—This element served the family of Noah in three particulars: First, it saved them. Peter declares that they "were saved through water" (1 Pet. 3:20). By means of it the ark was borne up and thus its inmates were saved from drowning. Second, it separated them. It divided the living from the dead. The believing and obedient were at the top; the unbelieving and disobedient were at the bottom. Third, it translated them. By means of it they were brought out of the old world of sin and corruption into a new world cleansed by the flood.

The apostle in his explanation of the type says, "After a true likeness (antitype) doth now save you, even baptism" (1 Pet. 3:21). Paul agrees with him by saying that God "saved us through the washing of regeneration" (Titus 3:5). As the "eight souls" of the type were not saved before or after the flood, but while the water supported the ark, so salvation from sin is accomplished in baptism, not before or after the act. And as cleansing anything is not effected before or after washing but in the act, so cleansing from sin is consummated "through the washing of regeneration," for then the blood of Christ is applied.

5. *Unity.*—This characteristic of the type is manifest from several angles. All the persons preserved from drowning were saved in the same way. They were all members of the same family and were held together by the family bond. Even in name they were one, for they were all Noahs. These facts were not accidental, as will be seen in the antitype.

The New Testament church was marked by unity. All of its members were saved in the same way, there being no distinction between Jews and Gentiles, master and slave, bondman and freeman. They were also one in name, for all "were called Christians" (Acts 11:26), a name derived from Him whom they followed. As a family of God, they were held together by "the unity of the Spirit in the bond of peace" (Eph. 4:3). Of them it was written, "And the multitude of them that believed were of one heart and soul" (Acts 4:32).

6. *Covenant.*—It is noteworthy that in connection with the salvation in type Jehovah entered into a covenant with Noah and confirmed it by the bow in the cloud. That constituted Noah and his family a covenant people, subject to divine mercy and blessings.

In like manner, Christians are a covenant people. As members of the new covenant, God has said to them, "I will be merciful to their iniquities, and their sins will I remember no more" (Heb. 8:12). The Holy Spirit is their guest, their daily needs are supplied, heaven is their home. This covenant has been confirmed by the blood of Christ (Luke 22:20), and thus he has "become the surety [bondsman] of a better covenant" (Heb. 7:22).

This study reveals the fundamental facts concerning salvation from sin. The kindness of God is extended to needy humanity, so that in apostolic language we can say, "According to his mercy he saved us." The inadequacy of human reason in devising a way of salvation is made evident, for had Noah been guided by his intellect alone, he would have seen no need for an ark on dry land. God's revelation was needed. Absolute obedience to the revealed will of God is a necessity in order to escape the impending destruction resulting from sin.

V

ABRAHAM

The original name of this typical character, Abram, was changed by Jehovah to Abraham, meaning a father of a multitude. That made him a representative man of both Jews and Gentiles. According to covenant, recorded in Genesis 12:1-3, Jehovah said to him, "I will make of thee a great nation," fulfilled in the Hebrew people, "and in thee shall all the families of the earth be blessed," made good in Christ. Paul calls Abraham "the father of all them that believe" (Rom. 4:11) and in so saying the apostle made him a type of all believers in Christ, whether Jews or Gentiles. His call, faith, character, and doings contain much needed instruction for the people of God in our day.

1. *His call.* Genesis 12:1-3—

a) Divine and verbal.—"Jehovah said unto Abram." In this he was highly favored of Jehovah, and the call came to him in such a manner as to be easily and perfectly understood. It was addressed to his intelligence, not to his feelings.

Like Abraham, people are now called of God through the gospel "to the obtaining of the glory of our Lord Jesus Christ" (2 Thess. 2:13, 14). Everyone to whom this call comes should feel highly honored. Furthermore, this call is perfectly intelligible for "the gospel," which means good news, is addressed to the human mind, not to blind feelings.

b) To leave the old life and begin a new.—"Get thee out of thy country, and from thy kindred, and from thy father's house, unto the land that I will show thee." That call meant for Abraham to leave Mesopotamia and the old life for a life of fellowship with God. He never went back to his people in the East. It was a break with old associates and surroundings forever.

Like of old, God calls people now to leave the old life of sin and its associates. "Come ye out from among them, and be ye separate" (2 Cor. 6:17). To be a Christian means a break with the old life forever. "We who died to sin, how shall we any longer live therein?" Baptism into Christ draws the line between the old and the new (Rom. 6:2-4). As in the case of Abraham divine fellowship was the goal, so now God calls people "into the fellowship of his Son Jesus Christ our Lord" (1 Cor. 1:9).

c) To fame and fortune.—Before his call Abraham had no renown, but Jehovah raised him to pre-eminence. He was elected as the fountainhead of the chosen people of God. This was great honor, for from them came the Savior of the world. By his faith he became the father of all believers in Christ, a position given to no other man in the sacred volume. Because of his fitness for the honor, "he was called the friend of God" (Jas. 2:23). Materially, he was greatly blessed of Jehovah. He was given the land of Canaan (Gen. 12:7), also gold, silver, flocks, herds, and servants (Gen. 13:2; 24:35).

The gospel call extends to all who answer it, temporal and eternal fame and fortune. The church is the only institution on earth which Jesus claims for his own and of which he is the head (Matt. 16:18; Eph. 1:22, 23). Its members are by him constituted "a kingdom of priests unto his God and Father" (Rev. 1:6). Therefore, to be a Christian is to be a member of divine royalty, the highest honor that can come to any human being. Besides, there is infinite wealth. For our material needs the divine storehouse is always open (Phil. 4:19). Spiritually, we are "heirs of God, and joint-heirs with Jesus Christ" (Rom. 8:17).

2. *His faith*. Hebrews 11:8-12—

   a) The basis of his faith.—"By faith, when he was called, obeyed." First the call, then the faith. From this it follows that his faith was produced by the word of God, and by no other means.

In the Christian Age faith rests upon divine testimony (Rom. 10:17). No testimony, no faith. In no other way has God ever produced faith in any man. From this fact we conclude that men should not be taught to pray for faith unto salvation, but hear and believe the gospel.

b) The strength of his faith.—This is seen: (1) In the problem of the journey. "He went out, not knowing whither he went." Not until he came to Shechem, "unto the oak of Moreh," did he know what land should be his (Gen. 12:6, 7). He trusted Jehovah to show him the way. (2) In the problem of the land. The Canaanite possessed it (Gen. 12:6). He faced a case of human impossibility in the matter of possession, but he did not worry. God had promised him the land and he trusted him for its possession. (3) In the problem of age. He was seventy-five years of age and Sarah was sixty-five when they were called out of Haran (Gen. 12:4). Abraham was one hundred years of age and his wife ninety when their first son was born (Gen. 17:17). This involved a natural impossibility which could only be overcome by divine power. Yet Paul tells us that he "in hope believed against hope" and "he wavered not through unbelief" (Rom. 4:18-21). In these particulars the strength of his faith is seen in that he did not doubt God's word.

In Romans 4:23-25 Paul uses Abraham's faith as an illustration of the kind of faith God requires now of a person to make him a Christian. He points out that it is a faith that does not doubt the testimony concerning the resurrection of Christ. When one believes that, he believes Jesus was the Son of God (Rom. 1:4). The conclusion of the matter is that saving faith must be strong enough not to doubt the word of God. No more, no less.

3. *His obedience.* Hebrews 11:8, 17, 18.—This is seen all along the way of his life, but is marked especially by two events which show the obedience of faith. (*a*) Leaving Mesopotamia for Canaan. He was called upon to choose between his relatives and friends, and Jehovah. But "he went, as Jehovah had spoken unto him; and into the land of Canaan they came" (Gen. 12:4, 5). (*b*) Sacrificing Isaac. By this "God did prove Abraham" to see whether he thought more of his only son than he did of God (Gen. 22:1). He stood the test, "accounting that God is able to raise up, even from the dead."

The same implicit obedience God requires now of all who want to become his children. Faith, in order to live, must act (James 2:26). (*a*) Christ must be given first place in our choice of associates (Matt. 10:37). Truth, conscience and loyalty demand that. (*b*) One's own preferments must be sacrificed (Matt. 16:24). When Christ has spoken, man's opinions are out of order. It is certain that repentance unto life, confession of his name and immersion unto remission of sins are commanded by Christ (Acts 2:38; Rom. 10:9). They are all acts of faith in Christ, hence styled "obedience of faith" (Rom. 16:26). For convenience Abraham could have decided to go to a mountain nearer home. And in place of his son he could have substituted a slave. But if he had done either, God could not have used him as an example of obedience, nor would his name be in the divine record as "the friend of God." People may now prefer secret discipleship, or sprinkling or pouring to immersion, or a human church to the New Testament organization, but Christ has spoken otherwise. Therefore in these particulars to refuse or modify must be willful disobedience. It should also be observed that there is constant proving of the Christian's life so long as he lives. When he has thus "been approved, he shall receive the crown of life" (1 Pet. 1:6, 7; Jas. 1:12).

4. *His attitude toward the things of this world.*—Jehovah gave Abraham title to the land of Canaan, yet he never considered a foot of it as his property. He purchased a burial place for himself and family (Gen. 23). His view of earthly wealth compared with spiritual riches is clearly seen in his relation to Lot and the king of Sodom (Gen. 13:1-13; 14:21-24). He refused to take advantage of the occasion. He confessed himself "a stranger and a sojourner," for he had his eyes upon the heavenly city (Heb. 11:9, 10).

By such conduct Abraham teaches what the Christian's attitude should be toward things of time and sense. Our Lord addressed his disciples as persons on the move (Luke 12:35). They are not to unpack and lay plans for permanent settlement in this world. Peter wrote to the church as "sojourners and pilgrims" (1 Pet. 2:11). Manifestly the present earth is not the promised inheritance and final home of God's people, hence they should set their minds "on the things that are above."

We now see the important factors in the divine program for a better world. Covenant, faith, obedience are the fundamentals by which God operates, and without these he does not advance. The covenant with Abraham was occasioned by immediate needs. The time had come when the founder of the Hebrew nation must be selected, the nation's home provided, and the world's future blessing announced. At the same time and in the person chosen, a perfect illustration was given of how the messianic blessing is obtained through faith and obedience.

VI

ISAAC

In Galatians 4:21-31 Isaac is paralleled with Ishmael in order to teach the difference between the Law and the gospel, and to point out the persecuting attitude of Jews toward Christians. That Isaac was intended for a type is clearly manifest in the words, "Now we, brethren, as Isaac was, are children of promise." In Hebrews 11:19 it is definitely stated that when Abraham offered his son, he "in a figure received him back." The only event in the New Testament this could typify is the resurrection of Christ. The fitness of Isaac as a type of our Lord will appear in the several points of analogy to be noticed.

1. *Miraculous birth.* Genesis 17:16, 17; 21:1, 2. —Abraham was one hundred years of age, Sarah was ninety and by nature barren. Under such circumstances how could Jehovah's promise of a son be fulfilled? That which was impossible by nature was accomplished by divine power. Hence we read, "By faith even Sarah herself received power to conceive seed when she was past age" (Heb. 11:11) and Isaac was born a child of miracle.

The birth of our Lord was also miraculous. According to Luke's testimony, the Angel Gabriel told Mary it would be accomplished by "the Holy Spirit" (Luke 1:35). Matthew's testimony is to the same effect, with the added information that Mary was with child before her marriage to Joseph (Matt. 1:18). This twofold testimony is sufficient to establish the supernatural birth of Christ.

2. *Divinely named.* Genesis 17:19.—God said to Abraham, "Thou shalt call his name Isaac," which means laughter. The significance of the name is seen in the effect upon the parents to whom Jehovah promised the child. To believing Abraham it was a message of great joy that in his old age he would have a son, hence he "fell upon his face, and laughed." The aged Sarah heard the same message with incredulity and from doubt she laughed (Gen. 18:12-15), though she later believed (Heb. 11:11) and rejoiced in his birth.

As God named Isaac before his birth, so he did his Son. Prophetically he said, "They shall call his name Immanuel," meaning "God with us" (Matt. 1:23; cp. Isa. 7:14). A short time before the child was born, God sent an angel to Joseph saying, "Thou shalt call his name Jesus," which means Savior (Matt. 1:21). He, too, was a child of joy, not locally as in the case of Isaac, but to the whole world (Luke 2:10, 11).

3. *Persecuted.*—When Isaac was weaned, his father made a great feast which aroused jealousy in the half-brother Ishmael who "mocked," or "persecuted" him (Gen. 21:8, 9; Gal. 4:29).

Christ underwent a like experience from his own people. "He came unto his own, and they that were his own received him not" (John 1:11). When he had healed a man on the sabbath, "for this cause the Jews persecuted Jesus"; and because he called God his Father, "the Jews sought the more to kill him" (John 5:16, 18). At last they succeeded in carrying out their malicious purpose by nailing him to the tree.

4. *Sacrificed.* Genesis 22:1-14.—"By faith Abraham, being tried, offered up Isaac" (Heb. 11:17). One night Abraham was roused from sleep by the voice of Jehovah saying: "Take now thy son, thine only son, whom thou lovest, even Isaac, and get thee into the land of Moriah; and offer him there for a burnt-offering upon one of the mountains which I will tell thee of." The next morning he began to carry out the divine specifications without complaint, remonstrance, or argument. The details involved will be brought out in the discussion of the antitype.

In the gospel story of our Lord there are many points of contact with the type. Isaac was the "only son" and the father was called upon to offer him. Comparable to this we read that the Father in heaven "gave his only begotten Son" (John 3:16). All God had he gave, hence "there remaineth no more a sacrifice for sin." Isaac carried the wood for the sacrifice. What a strange arrangement—the offering carrying the wood that should consume himself. The meaning of it we see in the experience of Christ: "He went out, bearing the cross for himself" (John 19:17). Isaac was to be sacrificed on the hill Moriah, the ancient location of Jerusalem (2 Chron. 3:1). Analogous to this, Jesus was crucified on Golgotha's hill in the same locality of the type (John 19:17, 18). In submission to his father's will, Isaac allowed himself to be bound and placed upon the altar. By so doing he portrayed the submission of Jesus to his Father's will and the surrender to the mob for crucifixion (Matt. 26:39; John 18:4, 5; cp. Isa. 53:7). "On the third day" Abraham arrived at the place for the sacrifice, and on that day "in figure" he received his son back from the dead (Heb. 11:19). In his father's purpose he was figuratively sacrificed and through divine intervention he was figuratively raised from the dead. On the third day the Savior was raised from the dead. He was literally sacrificed and actually raised. Abraham offered a ram as a substitute for his son, so that the sacrifice on that occasion turned out to be substitutionary. The great gospel fact concerning our Lord is that in death he was a substitute "for the life of the world" (John 6:51; 2 Cor. 5:14).

In this wonderful combination of events we see on the one hand the Author of the universe planning and directing affairs on earth, and on the other hand the willing co-operation of simple faith.

An aged couple are given their hearts' desire for a son who is providentially used to portray the story of the Messiah and the glories that should follow. Once more we are impressed with the fact that "the wages of sin is death" and that there is such a thing as vicarious suffering.

VII

MELCHIZEDEK

The only available history of Melchizedek is found in Genesis 14:18-20. The relation between him and Christ as type and antitype is discussed in the Epistle to the Hebrews. In 5:6 the author quotes Psalm 110:4 in which David's Lord (vs. 1) is by Jehovah declared a priest "after the order of Melchizedek." "Order" means manner, or likeness in official dignity. Therefore, since Melchizedek was both king and priest, the Messiah will be a King-priest. In Hebrews 7:1-10 the writer mentions some matters of historical and personal interest relative to Melchizedek which are intended as points of comparison between him and Christ.

1. *"Priest of God Most High."*—From this title and office we are to understand that Melchizedek was called and appointed by Jehovah. In official position he appears in the Scriptures as the first public priest. Before him and in his time the head of the family acted as priest, but this man was elevated above them all in that he was priest for all, as he was king over all.

In these matters he prefigured the Christ who also was called of God and appointed by him. He "glorified not himself to be made a high priest," but was "named of God" (Heb. 5:5, 10). Like the type, Jesus is also priest for all, for "he became unto all them that obey him the author of eternal salvation" (Heb. 5:9).

2. *"King of righteousness."*—That is the meaning of Melchizedek. In Genesis he appears in contrast with the king of Sodom, ruler over a people unsurpassed in wickedness. Because he swayed the scepter of righteousness, he must have been an outstanding ruler in that age of unrighteous kings and corrupt governments. To him the people came with their difficulties and misunderstandings, and he gave them a righteous decision without partiality. Him they trusted as counsellor, ruler, and judge.

Righteousness is also the characteristic of the Messiah's reign. God said of him, "The scepter of uprightness is the scepter of thy kingdom. Thou hast loved righteousness and hated iniquity." For that reason he was anointed and crowned king. We may conclude that corruption in government and injustice to the governed will never cease until our Lord's reign shall become universal. Then "he will judge the people with righteousness," and "deliver the needy when he crieth" (Ps. 72: 2, 12).

3. *"King of Salem."*—Salem means peace. Therefore as king and ruler over men, Melchizedek was a peacemaker. Being king of righteousness, he was qualified for peacemaking. "And the work of righteousness shall be peace; and the effect of righteousness, quietness and confidence for ever"

(Isa. 32:17). People at variance would seek his counsel and come to him with their troubles, thus peace was restored. In this he differed from all other earthly rulers. Instead of peacemakers, they were peace disturbers.

As a peacemaker, our Lord is especially distinguished from all earthly rulers. According to Isaiah 9:6, one of his names is "Prince of Peace." The way he brings about peace is by being enthroned in the individual life. First, it "is Christ in you" (Col. 1:27). Then he says, "My peace I give unto you: not as the world giveth, give I unto you." "Love your enemies" (John 14:27; Matt. 5:44). President Grant in his message to Congress in 1873 said: "I am disposed to believe that the Author of the universe is preparing the world to become a single nation, speaking the same language, which will render armies and navies superfluous." When Christ is invited to the conference table of the nations, they shall not "learn war any more."

4. "*Without father, without mother.*"—Among Greeks, Romans, and Jews it was customary to say that a person was without parents when their names were not known. "So Philo calls Sarah 'without mother,' because her mother is not mentioned, and Scipio addressed the mob in the forum as 'you who have no father or mother' " (F. W. Farrar, *Texts Explained*). No doubt Paul means

for us to take the same view of Melchizedek, since there is not a word in the Bible concerning his parents.

Jesus is also without any known spiritual parentage. Of him we read that "in the beginning was the Word" (John 1:1), "whose goings forth are from of old, from everlasting" (Mic. 5:2). These passages lead us to understand that he always was and evermore shall be. In the matter of eternal existence he is like Jehovah himself, for both of them say, "I am the Alpha and the Omega, the first and the last, the beginning and the end" (Rev. 22:13; cp. 1:8). Such language concerning the Ruler of the universe gives assurance that he will direct all events and carry on until "the kingdom of the world is become the kingdom of our Lord, and of his Christ" (Rev. 11:15).

5. *"Without genealogy."*—This expression, according to its Greek antecedent, means without pedigree, and is applied to either ancestors or descendants. Melchizedek is presented without father, without mother, without pedigree. He comes into view without parents and disappears without posterity. He had no predecessor and no successor. He stands alone as a priest of God Most High for all men.

In this respect our High Priest is like the type. "His generation, who shall declare?" (Acts 8:33.) Here the original for "generation" is the same word used with Melchizedek in the Hebrew letter.

According to the flesh our Lord had no descendants, the reason assigned being, "for his life was taken from the earth." It is remarkable that, with other prophetic facts relative to his personality and history, this of no posterity should be taken into account. Furthermore, like the type, in office he has no predecessor or successor. He alone is Priest of God Most High who can officiate with reference to the sins of the world. Therefore all human priests are impostors and usurpers.

6. *"Having neither beginning of days nor end of life."*—The Bible contains no records of Melchizedek's birth or death. He disappears as suddenly as he appears. For this reason he "abideth a priest continually." As there is nothing said of his death, so there is nothing said of the end of his priesthood.

In this he was "made like unto the Son of God." His priesthood is "not after the law of a carnal commandment, but after the power of an endless life . . . a priest for ever" (Heb. 7:16, 17). Because his priesthood is eternal, "he is able to save to the uttermost them that draw near unto God through him, seeing he ever liveth to make intercession for them" (vs. 25).

7. *"Consider how great this man was."*—His greatness is seen: (a) In the tithe. According to Genesis 14, this was given by Abraham as an expression of gratitude to God for victory over enemies. At the same time the sons of Levi, recipi-

ents of tithes but yet unborn, gave the tenth through their great-grandfather Abraham. This lifted Melchizedek above the Levitical priesthood. (b) In the blessing. This was material and spiritual. Melchizedek gave Abraham "bread and wine" and blessed him in the name of God Most High. Since "the less is blessed of the better," he appears superior to Abraham and also performs the office of a benefactor.

How great is Jesus? (a) As Melchizedek was greater than the Levitical priesthood, so Christ is after a higher order than Aaron (vs. 11). And "the priesthood being changed, there is made of necessity a change of the law" upon which the priesthood was founded (vs. 12). Therefore Jesus, on account of his greatness, not only ended the Jewish priesthood but also abolished the Law of Moses (Col. 2:14-17). (b) As Melchizedek blessed Abraham, so Christ has blessed the world. "Because of its weakness and unprofitableness" the Mosaic law "made nothing perfect" (vss. 18, 19). But "what the law could not do, in that it was weak through the flesh, God, sending his own Son in the likeness of sinful flesh and for sin, condemned sin in the flesh" (Rom. 8:3). Thus he enables all who receive him to become "children of God: and if children, then heirs; heirs of God, and joint-heirs with Christ" (Rom. 8:16, 17).

In several particulars we have seen Melchizedek "made like unto the Son of God." In office both are king-priests. In character and conduct righteousness, the aim of divine government, is magnified. In service there is self-giving for the peace and happiness of men. The eternity of their personality is a pledge of success and permanence of the divine program for the world.

VIII

JOSEPH

In the history of the Hebrew people Joseph is presented as a man of divine providence. In his explanation to his brethren of his presence in Egypt he said, "God did send me before you to preserve life. So now it was not you that sent me hither, but God" (Gen. 45:5, 8). This is also the estimate of him in Psalm 105:17 and Acts 7:9. His remarkable wisdom, the hatred and sale of him by his brethren, his resisting temptation, his degradation and exaltation, and the saving of his people make him a fitting type of Christ.

1. *His humiliation—*

  a) Hated by his brethren, Genesis 37:1-11.— This hatred was generated by several causes. (1) Joseph took account of the evil his brethren did and reported the same to his father (vs. 2). When he saw their wicked conduct, his righteous soul was vexed. (2) The coat of many colors (vss. 3, 4). Joseph was the older of the two sons of Jacob by his beloved Rachel, and being the son of his old age, Jacob loved him more than the other sons, the token of which was the distinctive garment. For this his brethren hated him and could not speak peaceably to him. (3) His dreams (vss. 5-11). In character they were dreams of power and authority over his own people, and as such they were prophetic of his future position according to divine arrangement. On account of these dreams his brethren hated him yet more.

Jesus also was hated by his brethren "without a cause" (John 15:25). Like Joseph, he took account of evil and came to remedy the same. This drew the hatred of the world "because," said he, "I testify of it, that its works are evil" (John 7:7). As Joseph's brethren envied him because of his father's love and plotted his destruction, so the chief priests and the Pharisees were jealous of Jesus because of his popularity with the people. They said, "If we let him thus alone, all men will believe on him" (John 11:48). Even Pilate understood this, "For he knew that for envy they had delivered him up" (Matt. 27:18). Finally, as Joseph's brethren hated him because of his dreams of power and "conspired against him to slay him," so the rulers of the Jews hated Jesus because he claimed to be Son of God and king and they plotted against his life. On account of these claims they said, "He is worthy of death," and called upon Pilate to "crucify him" (Matt. 26: 63-66; John 19:15).

b) Sold for the price of a slave, Genesis 37: 18-28.—The effective pleas of Joseph's two brothers, Reuben and Judah, averted the original purpose of taking his life. God had so arranged matters that at that time there passed a caravan of Ishmaelite traders on their way to Egypt, and to them Joseph's brethren sold him into slavery for twenty pieces of silver.

Our Lord also was sold for the price of a slave. The circumstances which led to his disposal were peculiar in combination. As in the case of Joseph, Jesus was "delivered up by the determinate counsel and foreknowledge of God" (Acts 2:23). Satan selected Judas as the instrument for the deed (John 13:2, 27). The motive of avarice, in conjunction with satanic agency, led Judas to betray Jesus for thirty pieces of silver, the price of a slave (Matt. 26:15; Exod. 21:32). In type and antitype the transaction was a commercial proposition. To such an extent were Joseph and Jesus despised by their brethren.

c) Tempted and tried, Genesis 39:7-20; 40.— First Satan humiliated Joseph through Potiphar's wife, but he stood the test, for he said unto her, "How can I do this great wickedness, and sin against God?" Although he was guiltless, he was put in prison and numbered with the transgressors. Next, Satan used Pharaoh's butler to keep Joseph in prison for two years through ungrateful neglect. This was Jehovah's way of testing Joseph's character, hence we read in Psalm 105:19, "The word of Jehovah tried him."

Like unto the type, Jesus was tried and tested. Satan tempted him in the wilderness of Judea; wicked men opposed him during his public ministry; Judas betrayed him into the hands of murderers; at his trial he was condemned on false testimony; in his death he "was numbered with the transgressors" and finally put in the grave. But through it all he stood the test. He "learned obedience by the things which he suffered" (Heb. 5:8). The judge who delivered him to death said, "I find no crime in him" (John 18:38). As the Savior of the world he was undefiled, and at the same time he demonstrated his power over Satan.

2. *His exaltation—*

a) Providential events which led to his exaltation, Genesis 40, 41.—The first event was the dreams of the chief butler and baker. Joseph's interpretation of them finally brought him to the attention of Pharaoh. It was the first step out of prison. Next, Pharaoh himself had dreams. Through his interpretation of them and by his wise counsel as to how to prepare for the coming famine, Joseph was released from prison and distinguished as a man of God. Pharaoh observed that his counsel was good and said of him, "Can we find such a one as this in whom the spirit of God is?"

Likewise there were providential events which led to the exaltation of Christ. The first event was his resurrection. He had been condemned on the charges of treason against Caesar and blasphemy against God. He claimed to be king over men and the Son of God. Of these charges he was acquitted when God opened his tomb and set the prisoner free. This was a demonstration of his divine sonship and holy character (Rom. 1:4). The next event was his ascension into heaven. On that occasion Jehovah sent angels to be the escorts of his Son (Acts 1:10). The fact that God received him proved to the universe that he was a righteous man (John 16:10).

b) His power on the throne, Genesis 41:40-44.—In authority Joseph was next to the king. Pharaoh said to him, "Only in the throne will I be greater than thou." On account of the famine Joseph was practically ruler over the whole earth, for to him all nations came for grain, and him they had to obey according to what he demanded (vss. 56, 57).

As Joseph was placed next to Pharaoh in the throne, so Christ was placed next to Jehovah in the throne of the universe. "He put all things in subjection under his feet" (1 Cor. 15:27). Only in the throne is God above Christ for we read, "It is evident that he is excepted who did subject all things unto him." Like the type, but on a much larger scale, the rule of Jesus is in effect universal, hence he could say, "All authority hath been given unto me in heaven and on earth."

3. *The divine purpose*—

a) To exalt one whom men had rejected.—That pointed out to Joseph's brethren the fact of their crime. They not only wronged their brother when out of hatred they mistreated him and sold him as a slave, but they also sinned against God. Murder was in their hearts, for they intended to leave Joseph in the pit until he died. But God delivered him out of the pit, and the prison in Egypt, and in so doing showed them their crime.

In like manner, when Jesus was raised from the dead and crowned ruler of the universe, God by these deeds pointed out to the Jewish and Roman rulers the fact of their crime. The decision of the court in Jerusalem was reversed by the court in heaven. This fact was announced by the Holy Spirit through Peter who said, "Let all the house of Israel therefore know assuredly, that God hath made him both Lord and Christ, this Jesus whom ye crucified" (Acts 2:36).

b) To produce in those who rejected him a sense of their guilt, Genesis 42:7-22.—This was accomplished by Joseph when he accused his brethren. He "spake roughly with them and said, Ye are spies." He demanded that Simeon be bound and imprisoned until they returned with their youngest brother Benjamin. This resulted in accusation of their own conscience, "And they said one to another, We are verily guilty concerning our brother."

There was a similar process by which a sense of guilt was produced in those who had crucified Jesus. Him whom God had approved they were accused of having crucified and slain (Acts 2:22, 23). This affected their conscience and led them to call for mercy in the words, "Brethren, what shall we do?" (vs. 37).

c) To preserve life, Genesis 45:5-8.—Death by starvation was upon the whole world. God not only sent the famine, but also the deliverer (cp. Ps. 105:16, 17). Joseph became the savior of the whole earth according to the divine plan thought out and arranged before the famine came. However, when Joseph's brethren sold him into Egypt, they did not know that they were executing the divine purpose, but thought they were carrying out a cunningly devised scheme of their own.

As the mission of Joseph was to preserve life, so the mission of Jesus was to give life. When he came the whole world was "dead through trespasses and sins" (Eph. 2:1). In the fulness of the time he gave his life "for the life of the world" (John 6:51). Like Joseph's brother, those who slew him did not know they were executing God's "determinate counsel and foreknowledge" (Acts 2:23), but thought they were achieving a smart plot of their own.

d) To render service without cost, Genesis 47:11, 12.—Joseph never charged his brethren anything for sustenance of life, and he gave them a life of freedom in Goshen, the very best portion of Egypt. But he charged the Egyptians for grain and they paid money, cattle, land, and finally gave themselves as slaves (vss. 13-26).

Spiritually our Savior deals with people in the same way as did Joseph. Concerning salvation from sin the invitation reads, "Come, buy without money and without price" (Isa. 55:1). "The free gift of God is eternal life in Christ Jesus our Lord" (Rom. 6:23). "No good thing will he withhold from them that walk uprightly." On the other hand, the persons who refuse Christ are in the same circumstances as Pharaoh's subjects. They are the slaves of sin (John 8:34) and all they possess, as well as their own persons, belong to Satan. It is a hard life, without personal freedom and pleasant prospects for the future. Sin is costly and its wages is death.

This interesting story furnishes another picture of the wonders in God's revelation. The most complicated circumstances are made clear by providential direction and control. A despised youth, subjected to indignity and temptation, becomes finally king and savior. The accurate parallel of Joseph to Christ, as revealed in the gospel, becomes a mental astonishment and at the same time a delightful contemplation. Who but the Almighty could design the picture and so perfectly blend the colors as to bring out the wonderful glory of the coming Messiah?

IX

ISRAEL

The Israelitish nation is presented in the New Testament as a type of the church. With that fact in mind, Paul addressed Christians as "the Israel of God" (Gal. 4:16). Twice in 1 Corinthians 10:1-11 he speaks of the chosen people as our "example," or type. It was necessary therefore that the history of the former should correspond to the history of the latter. Israel's experience in Egypt, deliverance therefrom, journey through the wilderness and rest in Canaan is a picture of a person first under Satan and then under Christ.

1. *The unredeemed.*—After the death of Joseph, "there arose a new king over Egypt" who set over the children of Israel "taskmasters to afflict them." They were made "to serve with rigor" and "their lives were made bitter with hard service, in mortar and brick." As a further affliction, Pharaoh said to the nurses who waited on the Hebrew women at childbirth, "If it be a son, then ye shall kill him" (Exod. 1:8-16). Israel's only prospects were hard labor and death.

This is a true picture of a person who is a slave of Satan in the toils of sin. To such a one Jesus says, "Ye are of your father the devil," and also, "Every one that committeth sin is the bond-servant of sin" (John 8:44, 34). He is made to serve with rigor for "the way of the transgressor is hard" (Prov. 13:15). In the end "the wages of sin is death." Therefore, like the type, the sinner is doomed to a life of hard work, disappointment and death.

2. *The redeemer.*—"The children of Israel sighed by reason of the bondage, and they cried, and their cry came up unto God." At that time there was a man of the house of Levi, Amram by name, whose wife was Jochebed. To them a son was born, called Moses because he was drawn out of the river Nile by Pharaoh's daughter. When he was eighty years of age, Jehovah appeared to him in the wilderness of Mount Sinai in the flame of a burning bush and said, "I have surely seen the affliction of my people in Egypt, and I am come down to deliver them. Come now, therefore, and I will send thee" (Exod. 2:23—3:10). In order to enable the Israelites to believe in him, Moses was divinely accredited by miracles (Exod. 4:1-9).

In like manner God has taken notice of the slaves of Satan and sin and has heard their groanings. Out of love and pity he sent his Son who said to the oppressed and afflicted, "Come unto me, all ye that labor and are heavy laden, and I will give you rest" (Matt. 11:28). In order to enable people to believe in him unto life eternal, God accredited him "by mighty works and wonders and signs," so that he could appeal to men, "Believe me for the very works' sake" (Acts 2:22; John 20:30, 31; 14:11).

3. *The redemption.*—According to the history in the Book of Exodus, Moses proclaimed to Israel a message from God (3:13-17). This they believed (4:30, 31). Their lives were spared by the blood of the lamb (12:1-14). They turned their backs on Egypt (12:40, 41). They were baptized into Moses in the cloud and in the sea (14:15, 16, 21-31; cp. 1 Cor. 10:1, 2). "Thus Jehovah saved Israel." Their gratitude for deliverance from the house of bondage found expression in a song of rejoicing (15:1-21).

The things which accomplish man's redemption from sin are of like nature to the type. The gospel of Christ is proclaimed (Mark 16:15). People are called upon to believe this message (Acts 16:31). Life is spared by the blood of the Lamb, called "our passover" (John 1:29; 1 Cor. 5:7). As Israel turned their backs upon Egypt and were baptized into Moses, so now the sinner is commanded to "repent and be baptized into Christ" (Acts 2:38; Gal. 3:27). The baptism in type got Israel out of Egypt and also destroyed the Egyptians. Likewise baptism into Christ delivers the sinner out of the power of darkness into the kingdom of God's Son (Col. 1:13), and his sins are left where the Egyptians were left—in the water. Then and there he is cleansed from all iniquity by the blood of Christ (Acts 22:16; 1 John 1:7). Thus

Jesus saves his people from sin. For all this mercy and love of God there is a continual expression of gratitude and joy (Acts 2:46, 47; 8:39).

4. *The holy nation.*—At Mount Sinai the Hebrews were organized into a nation. Jehovah became their king and they were constituted "a kingdom of priests, and a holy nation" (Exod. 19:5, 6). This form of government was not imposed upon, but accepted by the people (vss. 7, 8). It was the first government on record accepted by the consent of the governed. Their constitution defined duties to God and man (20:1-17), therefore the government which they received was a theocracy, a rule of God.

At Mount Zion the people of the New Covenant were organized into a nation with Christ as their king (Acts 2:36). They are addressed as "an elect race, a royal priesthood, a holy nation, a people for God's own possession" (1 Pet. 2:9). This government was not forced upon them, for the spokesman on the occasion "exhorted them, saying, Save yourselves from this crooked generation. They then that received his word were baptized" (Acts 2:40, 41). The New Testament became their constitution in which duties to God and men are defined. Therefore this form of government is also a theocracy, a rule of God through Christ.

5. *The pilgrimage.*—Israel's journey through the wilderness was made according to divine direction and guidance (Exod. 13:21, 22; 40:36, 37).

Providential care was given them in matters of food and water (Exod. 16; Num. 11:31-33; 20:11); clothing (Deut. 29:5); and healing (Exod. 15:26; Deut. 8:4). They were put under hardship in "the great and terrible wilderness" with its dangers and privations for the purpose of causing them to feel their need of God and to prove their faith in him (Deut. 8:14-16). War was a part of their experience and they fought the Canaanites, the Amorites and Og, king of Bashan (Num. 21: 1-3, 21-25, 33-35). God had promised to fight for them and this made them invincible (Deut. 1:30; 28:7; Lev. 26:8).

In all these particulars the Christian's pilgrimage is like Israel's. He makes the spiritual journey of life through the wilderness of this world according to divine directions (Rom. 8:2; Gal. 6: 16). In the way he is providentially cared for in regard to food (John 6:35; Matt. 4:4); clothing (1 Pet. 3:3, 4; Rev. 19:7, 8); and every other need (Matt. 6:25-34; Phil. 4:19). Moreover, Christ heals the wounds and bruises caused by Satan and sin (Luke 4:18; 1 Pet. 2:24). By means of temptations and trials the traveler is made to feel his need of God and his faith is tested (James 1:2, 3, 12). Enemies are in the way and he is compelled to "fight the good fight of the faith" (1 Tim. 6:12). It is a fight against the world (1 John 5:4, 5), the flesh (1 Cor. 9:27) and corrupters of the gospel (Jude 3). In order to win he has been divinely equipped as a soldier (Eph. 6:13-17), and the victory is certain through Christ (Rom. 8:37-39; John 16:33).

6. *The Jordan.*—When Israel came to the eastern bank of this river, Moses was dismissed as their leader and Joshua, whose name is Jesus in the Greek, was divinely chosen to "cause Israel to inherit" (Deut. 1:37, 38; Josh. 1:1, 2). Crossing the river was a new experience to Israel—"Ye have not passed this way heretofore" (Josh. 3:4). For that reason the ark of Jehovah went before them, so that they passed through the Jordan with divine help (vs. 13), and when they reached the other side, they came up out of it according to the command of God (Josh. 4:15-17).

In comparison of type with antitype we find that spiritual Israel inherits the heavenly Canaan, not through Moses but through Jesus, our Joshua. To that end he commissioned Saul of Tarsus to go to the Gentiles "that they may receive remission of sins and an inheritance among them that are sanctified by faith in me" (Acts 26:18). As the children of Israel shared with Joshua in their God-given inheritance, so we are "heirs of God, and joint-heirs with Christ" (Rom. 8:17). The Jordan was to Israel the dividing line between their pilgrimage and rest in Canaan. In this it was a type of death through which the Christian passes by divine guidance and help into the heavenly rest (Ps. 23:4). Israel's coming up out of the

Jordan by the command of God was a type of our resurrection from the dead by the word of Christ (John 5:28, 29).

7. *Canaan.*—This land, divinely prepared and originally promised to Abraham (Gen. 15:18-21) was offered to Israel before their redemption from Egypt (Exod. 3:17), and kept before them throughout their pilgrimage. It was to be their rest and inheritance (Deut. 12:9), a land "flowing with milk and honey." All of this was fulfilled to the letter. "There failed not aught of any good thing which Jehovah had spoken" (Josh. 21:43-45).

The heavenly Canaan has also been divinely prepared and is promised to the children of God (John 14:1-3). It is offered them in connection with their redemption through Christ, and is kept before them during their earthly journey as their future destiny. It is to be their eternal rest and inheritance (Heb. 4:9; Rev. 14:13; 1 Pet. 1:4). As the Canaan of the type was only for those who had been previously redeemed from bondage, proved faithful in the pilgrimage and typically raised out of the Jordan, so heaven is only for the children of the resurrection who have been previously redeemed by the blood of Christ, and who have proved faithful to the end of life. And as God made good every promise in the type, so he will in the antitype. Jesus said, "If it were not so, I would have told you."

Than this type, a greater illustration of God's interest in humanity the Bible does not record. A race of helpless slaves, in the grip of one of the most powerful nations of antiquity, is delivered by the mighty arm of Jehovah through a series of wonders which shook the kingdom of Egypt to its foundation and published abroad his name among the nations. The means and manner of Israel's redemption, their subsequent history and destiny furnish the clearest conceivable understanding of the gospel plan of salvation through Christ, of the subsequent life and its meaning, and of the believer's eternal fortune and destiny.

X

MOSES

In his farewell address to the children of Israel, Moses predicted a prophet like unto himself whom Jehovah would raise up from among them. That prophet would speak only the words of Jehovah, and whosoever would not hearken of him it should be required (Deut. 18:15-19). Peter in his sermon next after Pentecost quoted this prophecy and applied it to Christ (Acts 3:22, 23). That makes Moses a type of Christ as prophet. The term "prophet" as used in these texts seems to be inclusive of all the interests connected with the two distinguished personages, and the analysis which follows is according to this idea.

1. *Providentially preserved*, Exodus 1:15—2:15. —When Pharaoh issued his decree to kill the Hebrew boys in infancy, a number of agencies were employed which cannot be accounted for by human ingenuity alone. "The midwives," or nurses, "feared God" and refused to obey the king's command. Making the ark, putting Moses in it and placing it in the river were acts of faith (Heb. 11:23). Pharaoh's daughter, the infant's cry, his beauty (cp. Acts 7:20), his sisters —all were providentially used to save the life of this child. When he was grown, he had to flee from the wrath of the king, so "by faith he

forsook Egypt" and fled to a foreign land (Heb. 11:27).

The story of our Lord's childhood as recorded in the second chapter of Matthew is similar to that of Moses. Herod the king set himself to take the life of the recently born King of the Jews. To save the infant Jesus, several interesting agencies were divinely employed. The Wisemen were "warned of God in a dream" not to report to Herod the place where they found the child. "An angel of the Lord appeared to Joseph in a dream" and told him to flee into Egypt with his wife and the child. Again the angel appeared to him and told him to return to the land of Israel. Fearing the cruel and treacherous Archelaus, "and being warned of God in a dream," Joseph went to Nazareth in Galilee instead of stopping at Bethlehem in Judea according to previous plan. These events not only connect perfectly with the type, but also go far in proving Jesus to be the Messiah in that God protected him.

2. *Sent as a deliverer.*—As such Moses was fully qualified in character and conduct. "By faith" he refused the wealth and throne of Egypt, and chose "ill treatment with the people of God" (Heb. 11:24, 25). He was divinely commissioned to save Israel from oppression and accredited by the miracles he performed (Exod. 3:1-10; 4:1-9). As "God to Pharaoh," he executed judgment

"against all the gods of Egypt" and saved Israel by the blood of a lamb (Exod. 7-12). His final act in delivering Israel from Egypt consisted in taking them through the Red Sea (Exod. 14).

Christ as the world's redeemer connects with all the points in the type. He refused heavenly wealth and glory, so that "though he was rich, yet he became poor" (2 Cor. 8:9). While on earth he suffered ill treatment in order to accomplish his mission. He was sent by his father in order "that the world should be saved through him" (John 3:17), and to this end he was divinely accredited "by mighty works and wonders and signs" (Acts 2:22). As God, he executed judgment on "the prince of this world" (John 12:31) by overcoming Satan in the wilderness of Judea, casting out demons, shedding his own blood for remission of sins, and conquering death by his resurrection. In all these particulars he was "manifested, that he might destroy the works of the devil" (1 John 3:8). In baptism he completed the sinner's deliverance by translating him from the power of darkness into his own kingdom (Gal. 3:27; Col. 1:13).

3. *Officiated as lawgiver and mediator.*—Moses was forty days and nights in the mount during which time he did not eat, drink, or sleep with mortals (Exod. 24:18). While there in the capacity of a mediator he received Israel's Law. In telling them about it later he said, "I stood be-

tween Jehovah and you at that time" (Deut. 5:5). This law went forth from Mount Sinai in Arabia amidst a terrifying display of supernatural power for the purpose of proving to the people its divine origin (Exod. 19:16-19).

In official position Jesus is like the type. As Moses was forty days in the mount, so Jesus spent forty days on earth between his resurrection and ascension (Acts 1:3). During this time he did not eat, drink, or sleep among men, except on two or three recorded occasions when he ate with his disciples. As "the law was given through Moses," so "grace and truth came through Jesus Christ." Hence "he is the mediator of a new covenant" (John 1:17; Heb. 9:15). His law went forth from Mount Zion in Judea with such a display of the Holy Spirit that the peoples were "confounded," "amazed," and "perplexed" (Acts 2). This visible and audible manifestation of the Spirit proved to the hearers the inspiration of the speakers and convicted them of having murdered the Son of God. It was the first public announcement of forgiveness of sin "in the name of Jesus Christ."

4. *Worked as builder.*—The pattern for the tabernacle was drawn by Jehovah and delivered to Moses in the mount (Exod. 25:9, 40). The material needed for the sanctuary was freely given by the people (Exod. 25;1-8). The work of construction was directed by Moses and accomplished

by men inspired by "the Spirit of God" (Exod. 31:1-6). The purpose of the tent was that God might "dwell among them."

As builder Moses typified Jesus as the builder of the spiritual sanctuary, the church (Matt. 16:18). To him God gave the pattern with all its details, therefore it is called "the church of God" (1 Cor. 1:2). The material for this spiritual house is a people who offer themselves willingly to Christ. Jesus accomplished the erection of this building through his apostles who were inspired for the work by the Holy Spirit (Acts 2:4). The design of the church is that God through his Spirit may dwell in his people and through them do his work in the world. Hence the church is called "a temple of God," "a temple of the Holy Spirit," "the pillar and ground of the truth" (1 Cor. 3:16; 6:19; 1 Tim. 3:15).

5. *Served as ruler and intercessor.—* For forty years Moses governed the people as God's representative on earth. As judge he had the aid of seventy elders who were qualified for the office by the Spirit of God, and therefore could "judge righteously between man and his brother" (Num. 11:16, 17, 25; Deut. 1:9-18). As intercessor he had power with God. The first occasion was Israel's worship of the golden calf (Exod. 32).

Moses based his plea on three points: First, that Israel belonged to God because he had delivered them from Egypt (vs. 11). Second, that

God's glory in delivering Israel was at stake on account of what the Egyptians would say (vs. 12). Third, that God was in covenant relation to Israel concerning their inheritance (vs. 13). Though judgment came upon the people because of their sins, yet Moses prevailed and the nation was spared. For other occasions of intercession see Numbers 14:13-20; 21:4-9.

On the Day of Pentecost Jesus was proclaimed "both Lord and Christ," a position he will retain till the end of time. Like Moses, his apostles are associated with him in the administration of his Kingdom. Before he went away he told them that they should "sit upon twelve thrones, judging the twelve tribes of Israel" (Matt. 19:28). This they are now doing in that Jesus is governing the church according to their recorded word in the New Testament. He also intercedes for his people. When we sin, "we have an advocate with the Father, Jesus Christ the righteous," who "ever liveth to make intercession" (1 John 2:1; Heb. 7:25). The basis of his plea is that we are God's property, purchased unto him by the blood of his Son (Rev. 5:9), and that we stand in covenant relation to God in the matter of forgiveness of sin. On this ground we are invited to "draw near with boldness unto the throne of grace, that we may receive mercy, and may find grace to help us in time of need" (Heb. 4:16).

6. *Was a distinguished prophet.*—Moses was the greatest prophet Israel ever had. There were his brother (Exod. 7:1), his sister (Exod. 15:20), and the seventy elders (Num. 11:25), but he rose above them all. This is also true of him when he is compared with all other Old Testament prophets, for "there hath not arisen a prophet since in Israel like unto Moses" (Deut. 34:10). According to the work of a prophet, Moses should teach and predict. For this work he was divinely qualified and commissioned (Exod. 4:12; 24:12). The Book of Deuteronomy is an example of how he taught the Law of Jehovah to the people. The twenty-eighth chapter shows his ability to predict. He promised Israel prosperity and happiness if they would obey the Law, and outlined minutely the curses consequent on disobedience —all of which is confirmed by their history.

As Moses was the greatest prophet of the Jewish religion, so Christ is the greatest prophet of Christianity. "God hath at the end of these days spoken unto us in his Son" (Heb. 1:2). Attention to Deuteronomy 18:15-19 will make clear several items concerning him as prophet. First, he should be sent of God, "Jehovah will raise up unto thee a prophet." Jesus said, "I came forth and am come from God" (John 8:42). Next, he should come from the Jewish nation, "From the midst of these." This fact is proved by the tables of his ancestry in Matthew 1:1-16;

Luke 3:23-38. Moreover, he was to speak the words of God, "I will put my words into his mouth." John tells us, "He whom God hath sent speaketh the words of God" (John 3:34). Furthermore, disobedience to his message would bring punishment, "I will require it of him." Hence we read, "How shall we escape, if we neglect so great a salvation?" (Heb. 2:3).

The facts concerning his life will show that Jesus did the work of a prophet in teaching and predicting. Matthew, Mark, Luke, and John seem to exhaust the vocabulary in describing the effect of his teaching. The people were "astonished," "amazed," "marvelled," "glorified God," and "came to him from every quarter." His predictions treat of his betrayal, death and resurrection (Matt. 16:21), destruction of Jerusalem, his second coming, final judgment (Matt. 24, 25) and the coming of the Holy Spirit (John 14:16, 17; 16:7-11).

In Moses as a type we now see more clearly Jesus the prophet like unto him. It has been well stated in these words: "Let us search all the records of universal history, and see if we can find a man who was so like to Moses as Christ was, and so like to Christ as Moses was. If we cannot find such a one, then have we found him of whom Moses in the Law and the Prophets did write to be Jesus of Nazareth, the Son of God."

XI

AARON

The divine purpose in the Aaronic priesthood as a type is seen in the Mosaic economy which was a type of spiritual Israel, the church of Christ. As the type had a high priest, who offered sacrifice for the sins of the people, so has the antitype. This fact is further evident in Hebrews 5:1-5 where Israel's first high priest is compared with Christ. By attention to the office, dress, and duties of Aaron we shall see in him a type of Christ as priest.

1. *Induction into office,* Leviticus 8—

  a) The call, verses 1, 2.—Aaron did not take this honor unto himself, but was "called of God" through Moses (Heb. 5:4). Let men who have assumed the priesthood take notice of this.

Like Aaron, "Christ also glorified not himself to be made a high priest," but was called of God (Heb. 5:5, 6). To this call he responded, saying, "Lo, I am come to do thy will, O God" (Heb. 10:7).

  b) Publicity, verse 2.—It was necessary to present to the congregation of Israel him who had been "appointed for men in things pertaining to God" in order that they may see and know him. Thus they were impressed with the divine origin and authority of the priesthood.

A similar scene was enacted when our High Priest began his public ministry. There was a vast concourse of people on the banks of the Jordan when Jesus was introduced to Israel by the act of baptism, by the descent of the Spirit and by the voice of Jehovah (Matt. 3:13-17; John 1:31). From that time he was known among men as the Son of God.

c) Washing, verse 6.—This act marked Aaron's inauguration, and it was also a token of purity. By this outward cleansing he was made to understand that in order to mediate between God and man, he must have "clean hands, and a pure heart."

For the same reasons Jesus was baptized. His washing marked the beginning of his public ministry, and it was a token of his purity. Not that he needed any cleansing, for he was always pure, but to indicate his fitness to be priest of God Most High.

d) Anointing, verse 12.—This was done "to sanctify him," or to set him apart for the holy work of his office. By this part of the ceremony, Aaron was impressed with the fact that he was divinely separated for the task of dealing with men's sins.

In like manner our High Priest was "anointed with the Holy Spirit and with power" when he was baptized; thus he was "sanctified and sent into the world" (Acts 10:38; John 10:36).

e) Consecration, verses 22, 23.—The word "consecration" means a completing, a consummation, hence an entire devotion to sacred service. It was solemnized with blood, applied to Aaron's right ear that he might hear God; to the thumb of his right hand, that he might serve in holy things; and to the great toe of his right foot, that he might walk in God's house according to His revealed will.

The consecration of our Lord to the priesthood was not without blood. The crown of thorns, the nails, the spear were instrumental in staining his person with his own blood. His complete devotion to the Father in saving man from sin was evident in his life and death (John 4:34; Luke 22:41, 42).

f) Entry into office, Leviticus 9.—Moses delivered the tabernacle to Aaron who then began his work as high priest. This investment with priestly authority was accompanied by divine demonstration. "The glory of Jehovah appeared unto the people . . . and there came forth fire from before Jehovah" upon the altar.

In like manner Christ was given supreme authority in religious things (Eph. 1:22, 23). His priestly work did not begin on earth (Heb. 8:1-4), but in heaven on the Day of Pentecost. His entry into office on that day was marked by demonstration of the Holy Spirit (Acts 2:1-4).

2. *Dress*—

The sacred vestments worn by Aaron were exceeding lovely and very costly. They were "for glory and for beauty" and typified some moral and spiritual truths concerning Christ.

a) The white garments, Exodus 28:36-42; 39:27-31.

1) The breeches.—A kind of short drawers reaching "from the loins even unto the thighs."

2) The coat.—This garment was woven "in checker work," or squares, and reached from the neck to the feet. It was seamless, like that worn by the Savior at his crucifixion (John 19:23).

3) The girdle.—It was made of "fine twined linen, and blue, and purple, and scarlet." It held the loose robe in place and thus made the wearer ready for service.

4) The mitre.—This was made "of fine linen." Fastened to it by a lace of blue was a plate of gold on which was inscribed "Holy to Jehovah."

The personal characteristics made prominent by these white garments were purity and service. Holiness must qualify him who ministers in holy things before a holy God (Ps. 93:5; Lev. 11:44).

He whom the white-robed priest typified was "holy, guileless, undefiled," who "offered himself without blemish unto God" (Heb. 7:26; 9:14). As the girdle was symbolic of service, so Christ came to serve (Isa. 42:1; Phil. 2:7; Matt. 20:28). And even now he is in heaven as our service-girdled High Priest where he appears "before the face of God for us" (Heb. 9:24).

b) The colored garments, Exodus 28:2-35; 39:1-26.

1) The breastplate.—This conspicuous article contained twelve precious stones on each of which was engraved the name of one of the sons of Jacob. Within the breastplate were the Urim and Thummim, meaning "Lights and Perfections," i.e., perfect illumination, which enabled the high priest to receive revelation from Jehovah. The significance of the breastplate is revealed: (1) By its place. Being worn over the heart, it indicated the affection of the priest for his people. (2) By its contents. The gold and jewels spoke the high value of Jehovah's people. Moreover, Jehovah reveals himself through the high priest, as evidenced by the Urim and Thummim.

Just as Aaron bore the names of the children of Israel continually on his heart before Jehovah, so our Lord is "girt about the breasts with a golden girdle" of faithfulness and love for his people (Rev. 1:13; cp. 5). We are all on his heart, jewels most costly (1 Cor. 6:20). And as Jehovah revealed himself to the people through the high priest, so now God has "spoken unto us in his Son" (Heb. 1:2).

2) The ephod.—To this garment the breastplate was fastened. The ephod consisted of two parts, one for the back and one for the front. These were fastened together on the shoulders with two onyx stones set in gold, each containing six names of the sons of Jacob. The symbolic design was that "Aaron shall bear their names before Jehovah." Thus figuratively he bore on his shoulders all the people before Jehovah with all their interests and needs.

In like manner our High Priest is charged with all the interests of his people. He bears our sins, carries our sorrows and supplies all our needs (Isa. 53:4; Heb. 9:28; Phil. 4:19).

3) The robe of the ephod.—This was a blue, sleeveless garment, worn under the ephod. The skirt of this robe was trimmed with pomegranates of blue, purple, and scarlet, with bells of gold between them. The symbolism of this robe may be hard to understand, yet some ideas can be gathered. Blue is the color of heaven, purple of royalty, scarlet of sacrifice. Of the bells, "the sound thereof shall be heard when he goeth in unto the holy place before Jehovah."

The typical meaning is plain. Our Lord was a heavenly man (John 8:42), who laid down his life (John 10:15), on account of which he was crowned ruler of the universe (Heb. 2:9). His people are always to be within hearing distance (Matt. 17:5).

3. *Duties,* Leviticus 9—

   a) To offer sacrifices for sin.—These he offered for himself and for the people. The idea in it all is salvation by blood. Sin has death in it. Whatever removes sin must have life, for life only can overcome death. Illustration, the resurrection. Life was in the blood of the animal (Gen. 9:4), and since those sacrifices pointed to Christ, he is called "the life of men," because he removes sin by his blood. (See John 6:51, 53, 54). The emphatic words linked are "Sin," and "Death," "Blood" and "Life."

   b) To apply the blood, verses 9, 12.—As Aaron applied the blood, so also our High Priest applies his blood to the sinner when forgiveness takes place, and without the application of blood there is no forgiveness and consequently no life. Therefore, removal of sin is accomplished by the blood of Christ, not by the Holy Spirit. Moreover, the blood is applied on conditions. "Through faith" (Rom. 3:25); repentance, for it is "unto life" (Acts 11:18); baptism, for in that act sins are washed away (Acts 22:16).

   c) To bless the people, verses 22, 23.

   1) The occasion.—The blessing was conferred when sacrifices had been offered and the blood applied.

Christ also bestows blessings upon his people on account of his sacrifice. They are the forgiveness of sins, the gift of the Holy Spirit, peace with God and heavenly inheritance (Acts 2:38; Rom. 5:1; 1 Pet. 1:4).

2) The words of the blessing, Numbers 6: 24-26.—This benediction, in connection with the sacrifice and the application of blood, placed the name of Jehovah upon the people.

Christ, also, in connection with his sacrifice and the application of his blood, places upon his people the divine name. The time and place when this is done is in baptism (Acts 19:5), then his sacrifice becomes effective. Not until then does the divine benediction rest upon anybody.

The Aaronic and apostolic benedictions are similar in thought though different in wording (cp. 2 Cor. 13:14). "Jehovah bless thee" corresponds to "the love of God."

"Be gracious unto thee" answers to "the grace of the Lord Jesus Christ."

"Jehovah lift up his countenance upon thee and give thee peace" links with "the communion of the Holy Spirit."

In this brief attempt typically to "consider the Apostle and High Priest of our confession," we now see him more clearly in his relation to sinful man. His personal consecration, official dignity, and priestly functions assure us of his willingness and ability to officiate "for men in things pertaining to God." "Having then a great high priest, who hath passed through the heavens, Jesus the Son of God, let us hold fast our confession" (Heb. 4:14).

XII

DAVID

The history of David, the second king of Israel, relative to his birth, ancestry, selection for office, character, and achievement shows him to be a distinguished type of Christ as King. This fact is strengthened by covenant (2 Sam. 7:11, 12), by prophecy (Isa. 9:6, 7; Hos. 3:4, 5), and by fulfillment (Acts 2:29-33, 36). Like all human characters, David had imperfections, but in many respects he was as complete a type of the Messiah as could be found.

1. *Born in Bethlehem,* 1 Samuel 16:1.—The ancient name of this town was Ephrath or Ephrathah (Gen. 48:7), which distinguished it from Bethlehem in Zebulun (Josh. 19:15, 16). Later it was called Bethlehem, meaning "house of bread." Because it was David's patrimony, the New Testament speaks of it as "the city of David" (Luke 2:11).

The birth of our Lord in the city of David was not accidental. According to divine arrangement, he was to be "of the seed of David according to the flesh" (Rom. 1:3). Over seven hundred years before he came the prophet designated "Bethlehem Ephrathah" as the place of his birth (Mic. 5:2). Thus it came to pass that at the "house of bread" he was born who said, "I am the bread of life."

2. *Of the royal tribe of Judah.*—According to the story in the Book of Ruth, Boaz of Bethlehem Judah begat Obed who begat Jesse the father of David (4:21, 22). Of the chosen people Judah was the divinely selected tribe among the twelve from which the kings would come (Gen. 49:10), and David was the first king from that tribe.

Our Lord was also from the tribe of Judah (Heb. 7:14). This gave him tribal right to the throne of David. His legal right is established by Matthew (1:1-16) who shows that Joseph, the foster-father of Jesus, was a descendant of David and could therefore by law give Jesus the right to the throne. Luke (3:23-31) shows His blood connection with David by giving the ancestors of Mary whose father was Heli. It is significant that the two lines of ancestors are tied together in Shealtiel and Zerubbabel.

3. *Divinely chosen and anointed,* 1 Samuel 16: 1-13.—Saul was a king after the people's hearts, but David was a man after God's heart (1 Sam. 13:14). On this account Jehovah guided the prophet Samuel in selecting and anointing him. This should cause us to expect David to be a great king, and also to see in him a proper type of Christ.

Like David, Jesus was divinely chosen and anointed. Through Isaiah Jehovah spoke of him as "my chosen, in whom my soul delighteth" (42:1). At the Jordan "God anointed him with the Holy Spirit and with power" (Acts 10:38; cp. Matt. 3:16, 17). He also is a king after God's heart, expressed in the words, "This is my beloved Son, in whom I am well pleased."

4. *Manifested to Israel,* 1 Samuel 17.—The Philistines had come to Ephes-dammim to challenge Israel to battle. Goliath, a giant nine feet ten inches tall, was put forward, the purpose being to decide the battle by single combat. Israel fled in terror, but David accepted the challenge in the name of Jehovah. The victory made him known to Israel as the champion of Jehovah's people and cause. On his return with Saul from the slaughter, the women came out of all the cities with musical instruments, and as they played and danced for joy, they sang one to another,

"Saul hath slain his thousands
And David his ten thousands."

Jesus also was made known to the people in a remarkable manner. It took place at his baptism in the Jordan River. John said of him: "I knew him not; but that he should be made manifest to Israel, for this cause came I baptizing in water." On that occasion Jesus was pointed out as the Messiah by the descent of the Holy Spirit upon him in the form of a dove and by the voice of God who said, "This is my beloved Son." From that time he was known as the anointed of Jehovah whose will he came to do.

5. *Tested and approved.*—Because of Saul's insane and murderous jealousy, David was forced to flee for his life. During those years of exile he was exposed to constant danger, being hunted from place to place in the most desolate regions by his relentless enemy (see 1 Sam. 18-30). In this way he was trained, tried, and prepared for the position as king. He learned to put his trust wholly in Jehovah. He also developed a character of patient waiting for Jehovah's own time and of suffering every insult and indignity without retaliation. What a hard road to travel to the throne!

Likewise Christ, our king, was tested and approved. For three years and a half he lived a life of hardship and humiliating experience. Tempted by Satan, "yet without sin" (Heb. 4:15). Hounded by the rulers of the Jews who sought his life (John 7:1), yet he did not retaliate, but walked away from them (Luke 4:29, 30). He put his trust wholly in Jehovah so that he could say, "I am not alone, because the Father is with me" (John 17:32). A wanderer on the face of the earth, he "had not where to lay his head" (Matt. 8:20). Patiently he endured all sorts of privation and indignity, and finally laid down his life. Thus by the weary road of suffering he, too, came to the throne.

6. *A reign of righteousness and mercy.*—"And David executed justice and righteousness unto all his people" (2 Sam. 8:15). In Psalm 101 he reveals his purpose as to his own conduct and the character of his reign. The quality of mercy is well illustrated in his mourning for Saul and Jonathan (2 Sam. 1:11-27), his care for invalid Mephibesheth (2 Sam. 9:1-13) and in the forgiving attitude toward his rebellious son Absalom. To foster his religious zeal, he kept two prophets, Nathan and Gad (2 Sam. 7:3; 24:11), and two high priests, Zadok and Abiathar, heads of two rival houses of Aaron (1 Chron. 24:1-6). His constant delight was to "go unto the house of Jehovah" (Ps. 122:1). In all these matters he was a fine model for his people.

Like David's reign our Lord's is characterized by righteousness and mercy, only more so. Jehovah said of him: "And the scepter of uprightness is the scepter of thy kingdom. Thou hast loved righteousness and hated iniquity" (Heb. 1:8, 9). "When he saw the multitudes, he was moved with compassion" (Matt. 9:36), and to the sinful he extended mercy (John 8:1-11; Luke 23:39-43). His religious zeal was manifested in his continual teaching and preaching, his presence in the synagogue on the sabbath, and his cleansing the temple, which act reminded his disciples of the Scripture, "Zeal for thy house shall eat me up" (John 2:17). David made mistakes, but Christ is faultless. In all matters of conduct he left us an example that we "should follow in his steps" (1 Pet. 2:21).

7. *An invincible warrior.*—Jehovah said unto David, "I will make thee a great name, like unto the name of the great ones that are in the earth" (2 Sam. 7:9). As a conqueror his name has been divinely inscribed on the roster of the kings of Egypt, Assyria, Greece, and Rome. When he became king over all Israel, the first place he captured was Jerusalem which became his future capital and was known as "the city of David" (1 Chron. 11:1-9). He continued his wars on the nations round about until he came into control of all the territory promised to Abraham and his seed, and thus the word of God was made good (2 Sam. 8:1-18; cp. Gen. 15:18-21). In all his campaigns he sought the counsel of Jehovah who "gave victory to David whithersoever he went."

As David began his war in Jerusalem, so did David's Son and Lord. Christ commissioned his disciples to preach repentance and remission of sins "in his name unto all the nations, beginning from Jerusalem" (Luke 24:47). The remarkable story of the spiritual conquest of "the City of the Great King" is recorded in the Book of Acts. The campaign was prosecuted with such vigor throughout the Roman Empire that Paul could write in A.D. 63 the gospel "was preached in all creation under heaven" (Col. 1:23). Christ will press the battle until "all kings shall fall down before him;

All nations shall serve him" (Ps. 72:11). Thus like the type, Jehovah will make his Son's name great: "His name shall endure for ever; his name shall be continued as long as the sun" (Ps. 72:17).

With these facts before us we can now see the typical significance of David. Among all the Old Testament heroes there is no person at all comparable to him in character and achievement. It is only in the New Testament we find his counterpart in the "King of kings, and Lord of lords," who is now seated upon David's throne according to promise. "What think ye of the Christ? Whose son is he?"

XIII

GIFTS AND SACRIFICES

The Book of Leviticus, according to its title, treats of matters to be observed by the sons of Levi. It contains the laws concerning "gifts and sacrifices for sins" (Heb. 5:1) which were offered by the Levitical priests, hence the Jewish Talmudists speak of it as "The Law of the Priests" and "The Law of the Offerings."

The first fact about these laws for worship is that Jehovah spoke them "out of the tent of meeting." He had previously spoken the civil code from Mount Sinai. The prominent idea is that Jehovah alone is the legislator in religion and morals. Human legislation on matters of salvation and righteousness has not his approval.

The first seven chapters of Leviticus consider four kinds of offerings. They are the burnt offering, the meal offering, the peace offering, the sin and trespass offering. They were designed to picture our great salvation in its various aspects.

1. *The burnt offering,* Leviticus 1:1-17; 6:8-13. —The Hebrew word for burnt offering means to ascend. The whole of the victim, except the skin (7:8) was consumed by fire, thus in figure the offering ascended "a sweet savor unto Jehovah." Concerning Christ we read that he "gave himself up for us, an offering and a sacrifice to God for

an odor of a sweet smell'' (Eph. 5:2). This leads us to conclude that the burnt offering was designed as God's part in man's salvation, or the sacrifice of Christ in place of the sinner (2 Cor. 5:19).

a) The victim—

1) Within the reach of all. It must be a bullock, or a sheep, or a goat, and if the person was too poor, a turtle dove or young pigeon. The rich and poor met on a level at the altar.

The gospel presents Christ as a substitute in death for all men (Heb. 2:9; 2 Cor. 5:15). Before his cross "there is no distinction; for all have sinned" (Rom. 3:22, 23).

2) A male without blemish. It must be the best and most perfect of its kind, because the idea was to secure the perfection of the sinner.

The sacrifice for the world's guilt was a male, "a lamb without blemish and without spot" (1 Pet. 1:19). Because of His perfection He could be "the author of eternal salvation" (Heb. 5:9).

3) Divinely selected. Jehovah designated the kind of victim he would accept instead of the sinner. None other would do.

The offering for our redemption was heaven's choice. He is "the Lamb of God," who "chose us in him before the foundation of the world" (John 1:29; Eph. 1:4). "And in none other is there salvation" (Acts 4:12).

b) Disposal of the victim—

1) By the offerer.

(*a*) He presented the sacrifice "at the door of the tent of meeting." This was to keep him from idolatry (Lev. 17:1-9).

(*b*) He laid his hand upon the head of the animal. Thereby he transferred to it his own sins and made it his representative and substitute; cp. Leviticus 16:21.

(*c*) He killed the animal. Thus he enacted the penalty of sin which is death. In later times the priest slew the animal.

All of these things were fulfilled in the atoning death of Christ. As the victim was led to the sacrifice, so the Lord, without resistance, was led "as a lamb to the slaughter" (Isa. 53:7). The transfer of sin to the animal was typical of the fact that Christ is our substitute, and that "Jehovah laid on him the iniquity of us all" (Isa. 53:6; cp. 2 Cor. 5:21). The divine command to "kill, flay and cut" shows what befell our Savior when "he was wounded for our transgressions and bruised for our iniquities."

2) By the priest.—In order to bring the sinner and his God together, a mediator is necessary. This was the office of the priest.

(*a*) He applied the blood. It was sprinkled "round about upon the altar." Without the shedding of blood there is no atonement, and without the application of blood there is no forgiveness.

The good tidings to men now is that they have a divine-human Mediator (1 Tim. 2:5) and when he applies his blood to the sinner, his sins are remembered no more (Heb. 8:12).

(*b*) He burned the sacrifice. Not only was the animal to be flayed, cut and every joint dislocated, but in addition to this mutilation it was to be consumed by fire—the outward and the inward. The fire to be used on the altar was divinely kindled, never to go out (Lev. 9:24; 6:13). Thus was pictured the complete undoing and the fearful end of the unforgiven sinner. Sin calls for the destruction of the sinner by fire.

Christ, our sacrifice, suffered at his crucifixion not only in the outer man, but in his inmost spirit, Isaiah 53:10; Matthew 26:38; 27:46. In him then we see the terrible doom of the sinner, the destruction of "both soul and body in hell" amid "the eternal fire" divinely "prepared for the devil and his angels" (Matt. 10:28; 25:41).

(*c*) He carried the "ashes without the camp unto a clean place" (Lev. 6:11). The burnt offering was peculiarly holy. In life the animal must be without blemish. In death its remains must be kept from impurity. The idea conveyed was that the imperfect and unclean cannot secure atonement for sin.

The meaning of this part of the type is revealed in Christ. The purity of his life is impressively set forth. In death his remains were laid in a clean place, "a new tomb" (John 19:41, 42). Thus the fact is conveyed that only the perfect and clean can effect atonement for sin.

c) The design.—"It shall be accepted for him to make atonement for him." The word "atonement" contains two ideas:

1) To cover. This meaning is made clear by two illustrations. In Genesis 32:20 the word for atonement is translated "appease." Jacob thought that by covering Esau's face with a gift he would secure his friendship. In Exodus 25:17 the same word is rendered "mercy-seat," the covering for the ark. Since this chest contained the law of Jehovah which was often broken by the people, the idea conveyed was that mercy covered the justice and wrath of the offended God.

In 1 John 2:2 the word "propitiation" is the equivalent of the Old Testament word "atonement." Concerning Christ, therefore, we can say, "he is the covering for our sins," they are out of sight.

2) To be in harmony. The English word "at-one-ment" expresses this idea, which is the result from having sins covered. "We have peace with God through our Lord Jesus Christ" (Rom. 5:1).

2. *The meal offering,* Leviticus 2:1-16; 6:14-23. —The Hebrew word for meal offering means gift. It illustrates the second step in the process of salvation, man giving himself in service to God according to the terms of the gospel. As Jehovah designated the ingredients of the meal offering, so he has specified what the sinner must do to be saved; cp. Acts 2:38, 40.

The relation between the burnt offering and the meal offering was intimate and essential. In Exodus 29:38-42; Numbers 15:1-10 the two are presented as one and inseparable, and were consumed together upon the altar. The significance of this relation is explained by the gospel. It is on account of Christ as our burnt offering that we are moved to accept him, and identification with him secures life eternal.

a) The substance offered.

1) Grain.—The following varieties were used: Fine flour, or cakes baked in the oven, or fine flour baked in a pan, or fine flour baked in the frying pan, or first fruits of grain in the ear parched.

The typical teaching is evident. We are to offer to Christ the first fruits, the early years of our life (Eccles. 12:1; Matt. 6:33). Moreover, as the grain was to be the very best, so we are to give the very best and finest service of which we are capable (Rom. 12:1, 2).

2) Oil.—Olive oil was mingled with all the grain products of this offering.

In the Scriptures oil is symbolic of the Holy Spirit. For this reason Jesus is said to have been anointed "with the oil of gladness" which was the Holy Spirit (Heb. 1:9). The relation of the Holy Spirit to men is fully explained in the New Testament. In conversion they are begotten by him through his word (1 Pet. 1:23). They are taught by him what to do to be saved (Acts 16:31; 2:38). They are given the Spirit at baptism, and by the Spirit they are perfected in holiness (2 Cor. 7:1) for his name is "holy." Thus we see that the Spirit of God co-operates with man in availing himself of the burnt offering.

3) Frankincense.—This substance was a resinous gum, which, when placed in the fire, sent forth a very fragrant odor. The direction was to put it upon that part of the meal offering which was burned.

The New Testament explains frankincense to be typical of prayer (Rev. 5:8; 8:4). Since the meal offering was a type of man's part in salvation, when may he begin to pray? Saul was directed to pray at his baptism (Acts 22:16). According to 1 Peter 3:21 baptism is "the interrogation [literally, asking] of a good conscience toward God"; the soul's prayer for forgiveness and divine acceptance. It follows that baptism is the beginning point of acceptable prayer, which from then on through life is to rise as sweet incense before God.

4) No leaven or honey.—Leaven consisted of a lump of old dough highly fermented, and honey in that climate would turn sour. The prominent idea is the corruption in these substances, hence they were strictly forbidden in all offerings made by fire unto Jehovah.

We can be at no loss to ascertain the moral meaning of this prohibition as it applies to the Christian life. There must be avoided the leaven of hypocrisy and false teaching (Matt. 16:5-12), of sexual immorality (1 Cor. 5:6, 7), of malice and wickedness (1 Cor. 5:8). Besides these there is to be avoided the honey of sinful indulgence— the personal lusts (1 John 2:16), the deceitfulness of sin (Heb. 3:13), the pleasures of sin which last but for a season (Heb. 11:24, 25). Any and all of these will corrupt the offering we are to present to God. Hence we must present ourselves to God with a determination to "abstain from every form of evil."

5) Salt.—This ingredient is just the opposite of leaven and honey in that it preserves while the others corrupt. The eating of salt among the ancients ratified a covenant of friendship and faithfulness, hence "the covenant of salt" (Num. 18:19). To the Jew, therefore, salt with the meal

offering symbolized, among other things, friendship and integrity.

As Christians we are reconciled to God through the death of his Son (Col. 1:19-22; 2 Cor. 5:19). We are in friendship with him and he with us. Furthermore, salt is a condiment. The gospel is to be made palatable to the world by right living, hence our speech, as well as actions, must be "seasoned with salt" (Col. 4:6). Moreover, salt is a preservative. For that reason Jesus said to his disciples, "Ye are the salt of the earth" (Matt. 5:13). Without Christians and the church human society will end in putrefaction and corruption.

b) Disposal of the offering, Leviticus 6:14-23.—

1) Jehovah's part. A handful of the people's offering and all of the priest's offering was burned upon the altar. As "a sweet savor unto Jehovah," it spoke his delight in his people. As a "memorial," it centered the mind and affection of Jehovah's people upon him.

In the New Testament we are profoundly impressed by the love of God for his people. As a Father he delights in his children, and they are the objects of his mercy, favor, and constant care (Titus 3:5; Heb. 13:5; Phil. 4:19; Rom. 8:37-39). In return for his goodness we are exhorted to set our affections on things above (Col. 3:1-3).

2) The priests' part.—That part of the people's offering which was not burned was to be

eaten by the priests. In this way Jehovah provided the material support for those who ministered in sacred things. Aaron and his sons were to eat this food in "the court of the tent of meeting." This was also the law of the sin offering (6:26) and the trespass offering (7:7).

Paul makes this typical of the support of the gospel ministry (1 Cor. 9:13, 14; cp. Gal. 6:6). And as the priests were to eat their part in the outer court which is a type of the world, so Jesus made no arrangement for an ascetic ministry (John 17:11, 14). The convent and the monastery are not a part of the divine plan.

It should be observed that the substance and manner of the meal offering must be attended to according to divine directions. If there was deviation at all, God would not accept the offering. He means for his word to stand just as delivered.

How do we offer ourselves to God? We have no assurance of acceptance, unless we come according to the way of salvation divinely revealed. Note John 3:5, 7; Mark 16:16; Acts 2:38.

What manner of life do we covenant with God? See Romans 6:1, 2; Hebrews 6:1; 2 Peter 1:5-11. It is the doing of these things that secures entrance into the eternal kingdom.

Do we contribute definitely and regularly to the support of the church? 1 Corinthians 16:1, 2. Without this, God has not promised to accept anybody.

3. *The peace offering*, Leviticus 3:1-17; 7:11-21, 28-36.

The original Hebrew word for peace offering is in the margin of our Bible rendered "thank offering." To an Israelite it was a sacrifice expressive of praise and peace. In the New Testament its counterpart is that note of joy which always characterized the life and worship of the person who had become a Christian (Acts 2:46, 47; 8:39).

The fact that the peace offering came after the meal offering should be held in mind. Some teachers of Christianity have reversed this order. They direct the sinner first to secure through prayer and agony consolation and peace and then he may be baptized and received into the church. This is putting the peace offering before the meal offering. The New Testament teaches that peace and joy always follow compliance with the terms of the gospel. First, the sinner is aroused to a sense of his guilt through hearing and believing the Word. Next, he is called upon to repent of his sins, confess Jesus as Lord, and be immersed for remission of sins. Then, and not until then, can he offer the sacrifice of peace and joy.

a) The victim. It could be a bullock, or sheep, or goat, male or female, without blemish. Added to these were unleavened cakes mingled with oil. As in all other cases, this was worship according to divine directions. The worshiper appeared before Jehovah, not according to his own method and means, but according to divine revelation and requirement.

The Christian's peace offering of worship is also according to divine directions. It was just as necessary for God to reveal what constitutes acceptable worship, as it was for him to make known the plan of salvation. Christianity found man in heathenism and he could not know how to worship the true God. The church at Corinth furnishes an illustration of divinely directed worship in the use of spiritual gifts. The Holy Spirit directed the speaking, praying, and singing (1 Cor. 14:12-16). Now the Spirit of God directs the worship of the church through his Word in the New Testament.

b) The sacrificial acts—

1) By the offerer.

(*a*) He brought the offering with "his own hands" (7:30). He must not present his offering by proxy. From the first Jehovah informed men that his religion, in order to be effectual, must be a personal matter.

There can be no proxy in Christianity. This fact is overlooked by many, as seen in the use of godfathers and godmothers in relation to infant baptism. It is also evident in the practice of baptizing the living for the unbaptized dead among the Mormons. In worship the parents cannot act for the children, nor husband and wife for each other. Religion was designed to occupy the individual's intellect, affections and will.

(b) He laid his hand upon the head of the victim. The Hebrew word means to lean his hand upon the head, the idea being the animal slain would support or uphold him. Sin is a burden which will crush man, unless he is supported by sacrifice.

Christ is the sinner's only support. "Jehovah hath laid on him the iniquity of us all" (Isa. 53:6). "Cast all your anxiety upon him, because he careth for you" (1 Pet. 5:7). Without him to lean upon, one goes down in despair under the burden of sin and the ills of life.

2) By the priest.

(a) He sprinkled the blood upon the altar. To the Hebrew this offering was a sacrifice of thanksgiving because of the atoning blood upon the altar. For this reason the Psalmist could sing, "How amiable are thy tabernacles, O Jehovah of hosts," and his soul longed to be there (Ps. 84:1, 2).

Christians worship on account of the blood of "the Lamb of God that taketh away the sin of the world" (John 1:29). Because of the shed atoning blood, the hour of worship becomes to the worshiper a season of "joy unspeakable and full of glory." He longs to be in the house of God where he may contemplate the fact and significance of his redemption.

(b) He burned the fat, the kidneys and the caul of the liver. In so doing the priest presented the sacrifice as a sweet savor unto Jehovah. The act of worship thus became a connecting link between the worshiper and his God.

The purpose in Christian worship is to come into contact with God and to feel his power. This is accomplished by proper attention to the divinely ordained means of worship named in Acts 2:42; Ephesians 5:19. In "the apostles' teaching" we feel God's presence, for in the gospel is his power (Rom. 1:16). In "the fellowship," which means partnership, sharing, we are in spiritual fellowship with God and become partners with him through sharing our material means for the furtherance of the gospel (Acts 4:32-37; Phil. 1:5). In "the breaking of bread," which is also called "a communion of the body and blood of Christ" (1 Cor. 10:16), we come into contact with him and feel his redemptive power. In "the prayers" we are in direct communication with God who has promised response (Heb. 4:16). In singing we offer our sacrifice of praise to God from whom all blessings flow (Heb. 13:15).

c) The consumption of the offering—

1) The victim was shared.—Jehovah's part consisted of the kidneys, the fat and the caul of the liver. The priests got the breast and the right shoulder. Because the breast was waved from left to right and the shoulder heaved up and down,

these portions were called the "wave" and "heave" offerings. All the rest was eaten by the offerer who might share with his friends and the poor. Thus the peace offering became a fellowship of feasting on sacred food.

Christian worship is an hour of spiritual fellowship and feasting. Believers are in fellowship with God, Christ, the Holy Spirit and one another (1 John 1:3, 7; 2 Cor. 13:14). It is the enjoyment of the divine family around the gospel table. On this table are found the bread and water of life in the person of the Savior (John 6:35). Here we taste "the good word of God, and the powers of the age to come" (Heb. 6:5; cp. Matt. 4:4). It is a season of sacred fellowship and of feasting on the viands of heaven. Let no one mar this holy hour by offering humanly prepared food on secular topics. "Preach the word." Know only "Christ and him crucified." "Sing with the spirit and the understanding." "Be tenderly affectioned one to another."

2) The meat was eaten while fresh, Leviticus 7:15-18.—Because of the warm climate meat would soon spoil, hence the sacrifice must be eaten either on the day it was killed, or the day following. What remained must be burned. This offering was God's banquet for man, and it was not a feasting on stale food.

The Christian's spiritual food is pure and fresh every day. He cannot partake once to last him a lifetime. Like the manna for Israel in the wilderness, his nourishment is divinely supplied, but must be humanly gathered each day. He feeds upon the pure word of God (Matt. 4:4). He partakes of a living Savior (Heb. 3:14). He drinks from the eternal fountain; nowhere else can his thirst be quenched (John 4:14). Thus his "inward man is renewed day by day" until he attains "unto the measure of the stature of the fulness of Christ."

3) The meat was eaten in purity, Leviticus 7:19-21.—The flesh must not come near "any unclean thing," nor might a person eat it "having his uncleanness upon him."

The gospel is a holy feast. There is no concord of Christ with Belial, wherefore God's people cannot fellowship the ungodly (2 Cor. 6:14-18). They are to "abstain from every form of evil," and "from fleshly lusts, which war against the soul" (1 Thess. 5:22; 1 Pet. 2:11).

d) The time of the offering—

It was presented: (*a*) At divinely appointed season, such as at the consecration of the priests (Exod. 29:26-28); the expiration of a Nazirite vow (Num. 6:13-20); the feast of first fruits (Lev. 23:19, 20). (*b*) At any time as a voluntary thank offering (2 Sam. 6:17; 2 Chron. 30:22).

In the Christian dispensation there is a divinely appointed time and place for worship (Acts 20:7; Heb. 10:25). Moreover, as the thank offering of the type might also be presented at any time, so Christians are to live a life of daily thanksgiving and joy (Col. 4:2; Phil. 4:4).

4. *The sin and trespass offerings,* Leviticus 4:1-35; 5:1-19; 6:1-7, 24-30; 7:1-7.

The typical significance of the first three offerings needs to be recalled. The burnt offering typified Christ as the Savior from sin. The meal offering pointed forward to what the sinner must do to be saved from his past sins. The peace offering pictured the Christian's life of peace and joy because he has been saved. This traces the divine plan of salvation to a certain point in human experience. What next?

After a person's past sins have been forgiven, he still needs to be saved. Luke speaks of "those that were being saved" (Acts 2:47 marg.). Paul urges Christians to "press on unto perfection" (Heb. 6:1). Peter makes entrance into the eternal kingdom conditional upon doing certain things throughout this life (2 Pet. 1:5-11). Saving a person continues from his conversion to his death. He lives in a world of sin, and he himself is subject to sin. "The lust of the flesh and the lust of the eyes and the vainglory of life" exert upon him a constant pull. The tendency to sin is a part of his being (Rom. 7:17), and he does sin (1 John 1:8). He therefore needs a perpetual atonement. The sin and trespass offerings were designed to typify the fact that God through

Christ has provided for daily removal of sin. "Through his own blood he entered . . . into heaven itself, now to appear before the face of God for us . . . to put away sin" (Heb. 9:12, 24, 26). "And if any man sin we have an Advocate with the Father, Jesus Christ the righteous" (1 John 2:1).

a) The sin offering, Leviticus 4:1—5:13; 6:24-30.

1) The kind of sins treated.—They were sins committed "unwittingly," or in ignorance of God's law. So far as guilt was concerned, Jehovah made no distinction between unintentional and wilful sins. Both need atonement by blood in order to be forgiven.

The Christian doctrine related to this requirement of the law of Moses calls for attention. To the person born again the day of trial will come. He does not deliberately plan to sin (1 John 3:9), but he will be "overtaken," or surprised in wrongdoing (Gal. 6:1). He will "stumble" in many things (Jas. 3:2), hence an imperfect Christian. Like Paul, he is left to say, "Not that I have already obtained, or am already made perfect: but I press on" (Phil. 3:12). And like the apostle, he has a constant struggle with unintentional evil (Rom. 7:19). But the sin offering is available, and he can exclaim: "I thank God through Jesus Christ our Lord" (Rom. 7:25).

2) Gradation of sacrifice according to responsibility.

The priest must offer a bullock, the most valuable sacrifice, because he officiated for the congregation in sacred things. When he sinned, he brought "guilt on the people." The blood for his forgiveness was sprinkled seven times before the veil, smeared on the horns of the altar of incense, and poured out at the base of the brazen altar.

The congregation, because of its prominence, was required to bring a young bullock, the same as the priest. Forgiveness was secured by applying the blood in the same way as in the case of the priest.

The ruler, because of his public position, must bring a male goat, a sacrifice less in value compared with that of the priest and congregation. The atoning blood was applied to the horns of the brazen altar and poured out at its base.

The private person, if able, brought a male goat, or a female lamb. "And if his means suffice not," he could bring two turtledoves, or two young pigeons or, if unable to procure these, he might substitute "the tenth part of an epha of fine flour," the same to be burned with the animal sacrifices on the public altar. This secured for him atonement by blood.

Here is graded responsibility according to office. The enormity of the sin was determined by the rank of the sinner.

The lesson for our day is plain. More is required of the minister, the elder, the deacon, the Bible school teacher than of the private member of the church. It has been said that a public man is like the town clock, upon which more depends than upon the private timepiece. When a man's watch fails, the individual is misled but when the public clock goes wrong, the whole community is deceived.

In the New Testament this responsibility is emphasized. In the Lord's letters to the seven churches of Asia, it is "the angel," the messenger in the person of the elder, who is held responsible. James applies this lesson to teachers (Jas. 3:1). Furthermore, as seen in the congregation of Israel, there is also responsibility attached to an association of individuals. The church stands for some things in character and influence. It is "a holy nation" (1 Pet. 2:9). It is "the salt of the earth," "the light of the world," and like "a city set on a hill" (Matt. 5:13, 14). Because of her place and prominence in the world, the church must not teach doctrines subversive of morality and revealed truth.

3) The victim "without the camp."—The removal of the victim to a place not occupied by the congregation suggested that in some way there was attached to it reproach and dishonor. Since it was a sin offering, the idea conveyed was that there is disgrace in sin.

The writer of the Hebrew letter explains this part of the type as having been fulfilled in Christ (Heb. 13:11-13). He "suffered without the gate" as an outcast from the congregation of Israel. There he went bearing his own cross, a symbol of shame. There Jehovah laid on him the iniquity of us all. Thus the sin-burden of the world caused him dishonor and reproach outside the camp of Israel.

b) The trespass offering, Leviticus 5:14—6:7; 7:1-7.

1) The kind of wrongs involved.—The word "trespass" means infringement upon the rights of others.

(*a*) In things of Jehovah (5:14-19). God claimed certain things from his people, the withholding of which was a trespass upon his rights. Thus did Acham at Jericho (Josh. 7). Such was idol-worship (2 Chron. 28:22-25; 29:6). Withholding the tithe was robbing God (Mal. 3:8-10). All things that supported true religious worship belonged to Jehovah.

(*b*) In things of one's neighbor (6:1-7). Five cases of most common trespass against man are here named. They are unlawful use of a trust, or "deposit"; fraud in business, or "bargain"; "robbery," or getting things without value received; "oppression," such as retention of wages due (Lev. 19:13); keeping a thing which had been lost by withholding the truth. The sin of adultery fell in this class of wrongs, for the woman belonged to her husband (Num. 5:12, 27).

2) The legal requirement.

(*a*) Confession (5:5).—This public acknowledgment of his wrong established his guilt which led to the necessity of other requirements.

(*b*) Restitution (5:16). This included reparation for the wrong committed, in so far as it could be done, plus one-fifth. Thus the guilty person was not allowed even temporary advantage in the use of what he had wrongfully obtained.

(*c*) Atonement.—A ram without blemish must be slain before there could be forgiveness. As in all cases of sin, without the shed blood there was no atonement. Thus saith Jehovah and no man can change it.

c) Requirements of a sinner in the church. It has been observed that the sin and trespass offerings are typical of what a person must do to be saved, after he becomes a Christian. Attention to the New Testament teaching relative to this matter is now in order.

1) Repentance, Acts 8:22.—Simon the sorcerer was a baptized believer (vs. 13), hence in the church. But his old mental habits and latent passions overpowered him in the moment of temptation. Peter's direction to him as a disciple who had sinned was to "repent," and thus change his course of life.

2) Prayer.—The further requirement of Simon was that he pray the Lord for the forgiveness of his sin of avarice which characterized his old life.

3) Confession, 1 John 1:9.—It is plain from verses 8, 9, 10 that John wrote to Christians. He told them that forgiveness of their sins is granted on the condition that they are confessed to God, an act indicative of true penitence.

4) Restoration, Romans 13:8.—Paul's rule of conduct among Christians reads, "Owe no man anything" as a result of wrongdoing, for "love worketh no ill to his neighbor." Zacchaeus is a fine illustration of restitution (Luke 19:8). It marked the commencement of a new course of his life.

d) The atoning blood.—It has been noticed that in the type there was need of sacrifice and application of blood before forgiveness could be secured. The blood was applied before the inner veil, upon the horns of the altar of incense and at the base of the altar of burnt offerings.

In the antitype the necessity of blood for sinning Christians is divinely affirmed (1 John 1:7). It means that God cannot forgive anybody who does not avail himself of the shed blood of Jesus. But that blood is applied to the erring saint on the condition of his restitution, in so far as it can be done.

By means of these offerings and the New Testament interpretation of them we can now see clearly the things involved in man's salvation from sin. God's part consists in providing the sacrifice and giving directions which must be followed to the letter. Man's part is in the nature of personal, intelligent, and willing obedience in all things which God has commanded. Salvation, then, is plainly a matter of divine and human co-operation. The new life thus voluntarily entered is characterized by joyful spiritual fellowship, by purity of thought and righteous conduct, and by an impelling desire for spiritual service. The gospel makes it plain that one becomes a Christian and remains such, not because he is commanded to, but because he wants to.

XIV

AARON'S SONS

In a previous study of a portion of Leviticus 8, Aaron the high priest was considered as a type of Christ, our High Priest. The remainder of this chapter deals with the priesthood of Aaron's sons. In the Levitical priesthood there were two orders, the high priesthood of Aaron and the lower priesthood of Aaron's sons.

In God's arrangement, the sons of Aaron as priests typified all Christians as priests (1 Pet. 2:5, 9). The nation of Israel was spoken of as "a kingdom of priests" (Exod. 19:6), and so is the church of Christ (Rev. 1:6). And as there were but two orders of priests in the type, so there are but two orders of priests in the antitype. Christ is now the high priest, and ever will be, for he is "a priest for ever after the order of Melchizedek" (Heb. 7:17). Not some but all baptized believers are now priests of God. In these particulars the divine classification is different from the pretended priesthoods of modern times.

In the type the high priest and the lower priests had many things in common. First, there was the family relation. The high priest and the inferior priests were in flesh-and-blood connection. A like relationship exists between Christ and his people. He was a partaker of flesh and blood, thus made like unto his brethren (Heb. 2:14, 17). Next, there was the spiritual relation. The sons of Aaron became priests because their father was the high priest. This pointed to the fact that we become priests of God because of Christ our High Priest (Rev. 1:6). Receiving him through re-birth makes one a member of the spiritual family (John 1:12, 13). Moreover, in the consecration service Aaron and his sons were dealt with alike. Likewise Christ and his people fellowship in experience. He made the Good Confession, so do they. He was baptized, so are they. He was anointed with the Holy Spirit, so are they. In some spiritual things Christ left us "an example that we should follow in his steps."

It is also to be observed that Aaron's sons were all of equal rank in the priestly office. Among them were no inferiors and superiors; all were on equal footing before God and men. It is a noticeable fact that in the New Testament church there is no official rank, but there is official ministry. There we find no mitered heads or crowned overlords. Christ's people are not distinguished by clergy and laity, or by social standing, or by racial differences. All are one in Christ (Gal. 3:28).

We now consider the induction of Aaron's sons into the priestly office and the significance of its typical teaching.

1. *They were divinely called,* Leviticus 8:1, 2; Exodus 28:1.—This honor they did not take unto themselves, nor was it conferred upon them by human authority. God called them through Moses to obtain the glory of the priesthood.

In like manner, all Christians have been chosen and called of God (John 6:45; 2 Thess. 2:13, 14). The signal honor of the priesthood is not conferred by any human authority, but is divinely extended to every individual. The command is to "go and make disciples of all the nations." All who hear the gospel are divinely called.

2. *They answered the call,* verse 36.—At once, when God had nominated them for the priesthood, they consented to serve. No excuses were offered, nor was there any delay. Immediately they qualified by obedience for heaven's high election.

Not all who are called by the gospel to be priests of God make a cheerful and ready response. "Many are called, but few are chosen." However, on the Day of Pentecost there was an immediate response (Acts 2:41). Saul of Tarsus did not take the call under advisement but at once asked, "What shall I do, Lord?" (Acts 22:10). Cornelius of Caesarea and his household were anxious to hear the call and render immediate obedience (Acts 10:33, 48). Since the gospel call was first issued, there have always been some appreciative souls who have answered at once the invitation to become servants of righteousness.

3. *They were set apart according to divine directions.*—This is reasonable and to be expected. Only He who offers men the honor and blessing of the priesthood has the right to declare the conditions on which these benefits may be enjoyed. Any deviation from divine directions in this matter would make the subject a priest of a human system.

The following qualifications are demanded by Jehovah:

a) Publicity (Lev. 8:2, 3). Thus did Jehovah declare to the congregation of Israel the ones he had selected for his priests. The people were enabled to look upon the servants who had been "appointed for them in things pertaining to God."

The New Testament knows nothing of secret discipleship. Every case of conversion called for a public confession of the Savior's name (Matt. 10:32, 33; Rom. 10:9; 1 Tim. 6:12). Thus the person became a witness, a living public testimony, for Christ in a world that put a stigma on His name (Jas. 2:7; 1 Pet. 4:16).

b) Washing, verse 6.—In all ages washing has been associated with cleansing. In the type it meant that he who became a priest entered upon a career of holy living. Only as a clean man could he walk in the courts of Jehovah and handle things divine.

And what did this washing typify? The one ablution required of all who would enter the "royal priesthood" is in the divine language called "the washing of regeneration" and "baptism" (Titus 3:5; 1 Pet. 3:21). He who attends to it by faith in a crucified, buried, and risen Savior is cleansed from all his past sins (Acts 22:16). This act of obedience also marks the beginning of that life of holiness which must characterize the Christian priesthood (Rom. 6:1-4).

c) Vestments, verse 13.—After Aaron's sons had been washed, they were clothed in garments of white linen "for glory and for beauty." According to Exodus 28:40-42, the articles of clothing were a pair of breeches, a long coat, a girdle and head-tire. These "holy garments" distinguished the priests as a peculiar people of purity and honor.

The typical import of the priests' attire claims our careful attention. First, these garments were a type of the beauty of holiness and the divine honor which belong to the followers of Christ. "The fine linen is the righteous acts of the saints" (Rev. 19:8). The divine honor conferred upon them is that they are children of God and joint-heirs with Christ (Rom. 8:16, 17). In these respects the Christians are a peculiar people, distinct from the world, and the property of Christ (Titus 2:14).

Next, these garments were made according to divine specifications. So we must "put on the Lord Jesus Christ" in his own appointed way and live according to his law (Rom. 8:2; Gal. 5:22, 23). To assume the Christian life according to one's opinions of righteousness is to be without the wedding garment (Matt. 22:11-14).

Furthermore, it should be noticed that the garments were put on after the priests had been washed. It follows that a person is not a Christian in name and character until he has been washed. In the New Testament nobody is addressed as forgiven, justified, adopted, saved without having been baptized.

d) Sacrifices, verses 18-29.

1) The sin offering for atonement. Sin is ever present and needs atonement or covering. Christ is the covering of our sins (1 John 2:2).

2) The burnt offering for a sweet savor to Jehovah. "The wages of sin is death," and it delights Jehovah to provide a substitute for the sinner. Christ is our substitute in death (2 Cor. 5:14).

These two sacrifices make it clear that apart from the shedding of blood there can be no entrance into the priesthood. This is true of both type and antitype.

3) The consecration offering for devotion to service. Jehovah's purpose in the priests was, "that they may minister unto me" (Exod. 28:41).

To them the word "consecrate" literally meant to "fill their hand" (marg.). Hence Jehovah's meaning of consecration is for his people to fill the hand with service unto him, "and none shall appear before me empty" (Exod. 23:15).

This idea of service was impressed by application of blood. Upon the tip of the right ear meant hearing God's word. Note Jesus' teaching on hearing (Matt. 13:9; Mark 4:24; Luke 8:18). Upon the thumb of the right hand meant service for God. For this reason Christians are spoken of as bondservants of Christ (Rom. 1:1). Upon the great toe of the right foot meant walking before God in the path of righteousness. Paul wrote to Christians, "Look therefore carefully how ye walk" (Eph. 5:15; cp. 4:1, 17; 5:8).

e) Sanctification, verse 30.—Two elements were employed—oil and blood. The anointing oil was emblematic of the Holy Spirit with whom these who become Christians are anointed (1 John 2:20). This takes place at baptism (Acts 2:38), hence at that time one is inducted into the Christian priesthood. The blood which was sprinkled upon the person and his garments was typical of the blood of Christ with which "our hearts are sprinkled from an evil conscience" (1 Pet. 1:2; Heb. 10:22, 29). For other means of sanctification see John 17:17; Acts 26:18; Eph. 5:26; 1 Cor. 6:11.

f) Days of consecration, verses 31-36.—The number seven in the Scriptures is symbolic of completeness, and in this case it typifies the full and complete period of man's earthly life. The idea is that when one becomes a Christian, he devotes his whole earthly career in service to God (cp. Matt. 24:13; Rev. 2:10). As Aaron and his sons were to eat divinely ordered food during the seven days, so Christians are to subsist on a divinely prepared diet (John 6:35; 1 Cor. 11:27-30; Matt. 4:4; 1 Pet. 2:2).

In the consecration of Aaron's sons to the priesthood we learn how to "put on the Lord Jesus Christ," and what it means to be arrayed in his loveliness. The call to this end is definitely stated to be "the gospel." In no other way are people drawn of God. The response must be identical with the terms of divine revelation. God is jealous of his word. The ultimate aim is "salvation" and "the obtaining of the glory of our Lord Jesus Christ." With that in view Paul could say, "For to me to live is Christ."

XV

OBJECTIVE TEACHING ON SIN AND HOLINESS

In the offerings the cure of sin has been presented. The next step is by symbols to show the exceeding sinfulness of sin and the necessity of purity. This is the divine method of teaching, not only in the Old Testament, but also in the New. First, Christ wrought out our great salvation; next, it was published to the world. This order of development is illustrated by the parable of the Great Supper (Luke 14:15-24). In Leviticus 11:1—14:57 sin is exhibited in all its workings within and without the human constitution.

1. *Clean and unclean animals,* Leviticus 11: 1-46.

The purpose of this chapter is "to make a distinction between the unclean and the clean" (vs. 47), or to teach moral distinction. The operation of this law in the life of Israel calls for thoughtful attention.

   a) To separate Jehovah's people.—God chose the Hebrews from among the nations "to be a people for his own possession" (Deut. 7:6-8). He then separated them from the surrounding peoples geographically, morally, and religiously. This doctrine of meats was a mutual repulsion between Israel and other nations. For example, the

Egyptians held the ox sacred and never used it for food. It was not so among the Hebrews. The Phoenicians ate pork, the Hebrews did not. The Arabs ate the camel and the hare; these were prohibited by the Mosaic law. Thus we might go through the chapter and compare all its regulations with the practices of the heathen nations and we shall find no agreement. In all ages Jehovah's people have been dealt with as unlike all others. As we see it in the Mosaic age, so we witness it in the Christian dispensation. That the followers of Christ are separated from the world in character and conduct, is emphatically the teaching of the gospel (2 Cor. 6:14-18; 1 Thess. 5:22; 1 John 2:15, 16).

b) To teach holiness.—The various kinds of clean animals were intended to teach the necessity of a holy character in order to approach Jehovah. God's first lesson on holiness came to polluted man in the type of clean animals at the time of the flood and probably before (Gen. 7:2; 8:20). It was developed more fully by the Mosaic code. Sacrifices could be taken from the clean animals only, and such only as were "without blemish."

Thus in this ceremonial system with its distinction between clean and unclean and its divers washings for cleansing we have the meaning of holiness. It has been said, "There is demonstrative evidence of the fact, that the idea of perfect moral purity, as connected with the idea of God, is now, and always has been, the same which was originated and conveyed to the minds of the Jews by the machinery of the Levitical dispensation." It is certain that in the New Testament the Greek word for "holiness" derived its meaning, not from the classic Greek, but from the Hebrew Scriptures. And the fact is amply proved that the religious world has borrowed its ideas of cleanness, sanctity and separation from the law of Jehovah. This appears self-evidently so, for only the holy Jehovah could teach holiness to corrupted man.

c) To give a picture of the character of sin. The unclean animals were just so many living illustrations of the beastliness of sin.

1) Sin is unclean and to be avoided.—As the Hebrews were not to touch, taste or handle these unclean animals, so sin unfits man for fellowship with Jehovah and his people (Isa. 52:2; Ps. 1:1).

2) Sin is brutish.—It came to this earth through the medium of a reptile, and its brutal character is seen in the sinner. His understanding becomes brutish (Prov. 30:2) and he lives on the animal plane, being governed by his passions and appetite (cp. Rom. 7:18-20).

The several characteristics of sin can be seen in the unclean animals. This method of instruction Jesus used when he called Herod Antipas "that fox" because of his cunning and knavery (Luke 13:32). Like the camel, sin is ugly and spiteful;

like the hog, it is filthy and sensual; like the ass, it is stupid and stubborn; like the tiger and panther, it is savage and bloodthirsty; like the vulture, it loves the foul carcass; like the eagle, it sinks its talons and bloody beak in the innocent; like the fish without scales which creeps in the mud, it is slimy and abhorrent. By these animal symbols Jehovah has stamped sin as the abominable thing which he hates, and he calls upon all who love him to "hate evil" (Ps. 97:10).

3) Sin brings destruction.—As the brute is destined to perish, so is the sinner (Ps. 49:10). In sin there is death, physical and spiritual (Gen. 2:17; Ezek. 18:4; Rom. 5:12).

2. *Purification at Childbirth,* Leviticus 12:1-8.

The preceding chapter treated of the brutalizing effect of sin and the necessity of moral distinction. But what the source and seat of sin? How is it propagated in the world? The twelfth chapter gives the true answer.

a) Sin in relation to birth.

1) Sin and our original parents.—They were God-made, hence good and upright (Gen. 1:27, 31; Eccles. 7:29). Since the creator did not give them an evil nature, how account for sinful human nature?

"Through one man sin entered into the world" (Rom. 5:12). But how did it get into that one man? Genesis 3:1-8 tells the story. The Bible is the only book in the world that offers historical data concerning the origin of sin.

2) The propagation of sin.—The chapter under consideration tells us that we have come from sinful mothers, and it connects with the story in Genesis which relates the fact that "the woman being beguiled hath fallen into transgression" (1 Tim. 2:14). But the Bible also tells us that we have come from sinful fathers. "Adam lived a hundred and thirty years, and begat a son of his own likeness, after his image; and called his name Seth" (Gen. 5:3). Since Seth was born after the fall, the only reason for this explanatory statement is to make known the fact that Adam transmitted his own sin-affected nature to his son. The Bible and science agree that by the law of heredity parents transmit mental, moral, and physical characteristics to their children. This natural law is seen in vegetable and animal life which always produces "after its kind." Because the tendency to sin is transmitted by generation, David could say: "Behold, I was brought forth in iniquity; And in sin did my mother conceive me" (Ps. 51:5). This furnishes ground for the necessity of being "born again" when one has reached the age of accountability.

b) Sin as an unclean thing.

1) Separation of the mother.—After giving birth to a child she was dealt with as "unclean," forty days for a son and eighty days for a

daughter. During this time she was "forbidden to enter the sanctuary, to keep the Passover, and partake of holy food." This ceremonial uncleanness was a type of the pollution of sin. It defiles a person and separates him from holy fellowship and sacred things.

It should be observed that the mother only was considered unclean, not the child. The doctrine of "hereditary total depravity" which holds that a babe at birth is sinful and therefore needs to be baptized, is not of the Scriptures but of men. Sin is defined as "lawlessness" (1 John 3:4). Until the child is capable of wilful transgression, he is considered as an heir of "the kingdom of heaven" (Matt. 19:14).

2) Circumcision of the male child.—This rite was enjoined upon Abraham and his descendants as a necessary condition of Jewish nationality (Gen. 17:9-14). It was a mark of Jehovah's people which differentiated them from all others. It also served as a symbol of moral purity (Isa. 52:1; Jer. 4:4). As such it became a type of that moral and spiritual purity required of God's people in the gospel age (Rom. 2:28, 29; Phil. 3:3; Col. 2:11, 12).

c) The means for cleansing.—One significant fact about God's revelation is that when it speaks of the baneful effect of sin, it also points out the remedy. The mother, after a limited time of separation, could bring her offerings "unto the door of the tent of meeting" and the priest would "make atonement." Thus she was restored to her former social status. The important teaching is that sin has its antidote in sacrifice, "And apart from the shedding of blood there is no remission" (Heb. 9:22).

3. *Leprosy*—

a) Leprosy of person, Leviticus 13:1-46; 14: 1-32.

The Hebrew word for leprosy means "a stroke." As a divine judgment it was inflicted upon Miriam, Gehazi, Uzziah (Num. 12:10; 2 Kings 5:27; 2 Chron. 26:16-21). As a type it was singled out from all the ills of earth to illustrate sin in man.

1) The symptoms.—Three signs are named —"a white rising, a scab, a bright spot." These were small at first and not easily detected. For this reason repeated and careful observation was required of the priest.

Like leprosy, sin has a small beginning. It is first conceived in lust, next born in deed, then fullgrown in habit (Jas. 1:14, 15). "Sow a thought, reap an act; sow an act, reap habit; sow habit, reap character; sow character, reap destiny."

2) The characteristics.

(a) It is transmissible.—Leprosy is both hereditary and contagious. In either case it begins within and is at first unseen. It may remain dormant in the blood for years before signs of it are manifest.

The beginnings of sin are also hereditary and contagious. Blood tells physically and spiritually. We inherit from our parents the tendency to sin, and we do sin. "Through one man sin entered into the world." The evil that men do lives after them. Not only does blood tell, but surroundings also. We are sin-infected through association with men. "Be not deceived: Evil companionships corrupt good morals" (1 Cor. 15:33).

(*b*) It s p r e a d s gradually.—Although slight at first, leprosy is certainly progressive until the whole person is affected. His hair, eyes, nose, teeth and flesh are eaten away, limb drops from limb, until finally the victim is consumed.

In like manner sin is gradual in its development. A man does not become a villain in a day, neither can he stand still morally. He is continually going on, either unto perfection or imperfection, both in time and eternity. "Evil men . . . wax worse and worse" (2 Tim. 3:13; cp. Rev. 22:11).

(*c*) It is exceedingly loathsome.—Of all persons the leper is the most repulsive sight to behold. His face is sallow and death-like, his hair is dry and disheveled, his finger nails are discolored and tainted, his body exudes offensive ichor and odor.

What an impersonation of the vileness of sin! Isaiah used it in his pen picture of the developed sinner (Isa. 1:4-6). Wickedness is hideous; moral impurity is repulsive. Hence the morally and spiritually clean can but "abhor that which is evil," "and have no fellowship with the unfruitful works of darkness" (Rom. 12:9; Eph. 5:11, 12).

(d) It makes one insensible.—As the disease progresses, the victim becomes numb and insensible in the spots affected. In extreme cases a knife or fire may be used yet no pain is felt. This insensibility also extends to the mind. In the final stage, "the leper seems happy and contented with his sad condition."

Thus it is also with the effect of sin. At first it produces a keen pang of conscience, but after a while conscience is "seared as with a hot iron" and the victim becomes "past feeling" (1 Tim. 4:2; Eph. 4:19).

(e) It separates.—A Jewish leper was cut off from the congregation of Israel, from his family, friends and neighbors. He must "dwell alone without the camp." The law required him to appear with rent clothes, neglected hair, covered lip, and cry, "Unclean, unclean." He must assume the ordinary signs of mourning for the dead, and thus regard himself as a dead man.

As in the type, so in the antitype. Sin separates men from decent society. The church must withdraw fellowship from the unclean man (1 Cor. 5:1-8; 2 Thess. 3:6). In this life he is regarded as "dead while living" (1 Tim. 5:6; Eph. 2:1), and in the future world his destiny is "the second death," the eternal separation from God and all holy beings (Rev. 21:8, 27).

(f) It is incurable by earthly means. This disease was not treated by a physician but by a priest. Although modern medical science has found a cure for leprosy, it is effective only in the early stage of the disease. In the time of the type there was no known earthly remedy. Only divine power could heal the leper. (See 2 Kings 5:1-14; Matt. 8:1-3.)

The sorer malady of the soul is also incurable by human means. Legislation, education and self-imposed morality cannot heal and cleanse the sinner. The blood of Christ is the only "fountain opened ... for sin and for uncleanness" (Zech. 13:1; cp. 1 John 1:7). And when our High Priest says to the believing penitent sinner, "I will; be thou made clean," it is done.

3) The cleansing, Leviticus 14:1-32.—The cure had already been effected by divine power, still the leper had to do something in order to be cleansed. It was a case of divine and human cooperation. This is illustrated in Luke 17:14, "As they *went*, they were cleansed."

The typical import of "the law of the leper in the day of his cleansing" is what a sinner must do to be saved.

In restoring the leper, there were two distinct series of ceremonies. The first, which lasted seven days, took place without the camp, and terminated his condition as ceremonially dead to human society. The second began on the eighth day and specified what he must do as a worshiper in fellowship with Jehovah's people.

(a) The first cleansing, Leviticus 14:1-9.

(1) The priest goes forth to meet him.—By so doing he showed his interest in and sympathy for the unfortunate one. Moreover, the priest was vested with final authority in the case. He pronounced the person a leper, or not. He commanded what must be done in the cleansing. Jehovah by his law acted through the priest.

It is even so with the penitent sinner. God goes forth to meet him, illustrated in the father of the prodigal son (Luke 15:20). Christ, our High Priest, is "moved with compassion" (Matt. 9:36). He alone prescribes what the sinner must do to be cleansed, hence God has said to men, "Hear ye him."

(2) The process of cleansing.—The priest's part was to take two living clean birds, one of which was killed in a vessel over running water, thus blood and water were joined. By this blood the leper was sprinkled, the priest applying it with a bunch of hyssop and the living bird which were tied to a stick of cedar with a scarlet cord, and then the living bird was let go. Next, the leper himself must do something. He must shave off his

hair, beard, and eyebrows, wash his clothes and bathe his body. "And he shall be clean: after that he shall come into the camp."

In the light of the gospel this symbolic cleansing is easily understood. When the moral leper is cleansed, blood and water are joined. Jesus, our priest, applies his blood in the sinner's baptism, for then his heart is "sprinkled from an evil conscience" (Heb. 10:22). His blood is called "the blood of sprinkling" (Heb. 12:24; cp. 1 Pet. 1:2), because in the type the blood of the slain bird was sprinkled, not only by the hyssop but also by the living bird as it flew away. Thus in baptism the penitent believer is cleansed "from his old sins" (2 Pet. 1:9; cp. Acts 22:16), and he rises from the watery grave, where his corruption was left, "to walk in newness of life" (Rom. 6:4). He is now in the camp of God's people, the church.

(*b*) The second cleansing, Leviticus 14:10-32.

After the leper had been cleansed and fully restored to fellowship with Jehovah and his people, sacrifices were offered. They were not sacrifices of a leper, but of a clean person, yet there was a remembrance of sin. It is evident that in the gospel age this part of the type has to do with the redeemed man's life in the church, and that provision has been made for his sins after he has become a Christian.

(1) The several offerings.—The significance of each of these has already been explained and needs only to be recalled.

The meal offering of fine flour and oil was, according to its Hebrew word, the gift offering which signified the giving of oneself in service to God

The trespass offering of one lamb and a log of oil was for trespasses in things belonging to Jehovah, or against one's neighbor.

The sin offering of one lamb was for atonement of sins committed "unwittingly," or in ignorance.

The burnt offering of one lamb was the regular offering for atonement.

These offerings presented "at the door of the tent of meeting," the usual place of all offerings, indicate that the cleansed leper was enjoying all the privileges and obligations of Jehovah's people.

The application of this to the person in the church is not difficult to see. For his meal offering he is giving his life in service, "a living sacrifice, holy, acceptable to God." When he goes wrong his trespass, sin and burnt offerings he finds in Christ whose atonement is perpetual and available every day. But this atonement is conditional on repentance, confession and prayer, a matter already discussed under the Sin and Trespass Offerings.

(2) Provision for the poor.—Instead of three lambs, the poor person was permitted to

bring one lamb and two turtledoves, or two young pigeons; and instead of three-tenths of an ephah of fine flour he could bring one-tenth, with some oil, "as he is able to get."

The typical teaching is, first, that salvation is within the reach of all men. "The rich and the poor meet together" in Christ "who gave himself a ransom for all." Salvation is offered, not upon the basis of wealth, but upon character (Acts 10: 34, 35). In the next place, we are saved according to our ability (Matt. 25:15). This includes mental endowment, bodily strength and material resources—all of which are to be employed in Christian service.

b) Leprosy of garments, Leviticus 13:47-59.

The Scriptures discuss sin in relation to man's clothing. Sin uncovers the sinner and exposes him in shame (Gen. 3:7). It is significant that the self-made covering of Adam and Eve was not sufficient, so Jehovah God made them coats of skin (Gen. 3:21). Filthy garments typify iniquity (Zech. 3: 3-5). The same idea is associated with leprous garments. Since our garments are our immediate surroundings, the leprosy of garments was intended as a type of sin around man. In the antitype his environment is contemplated as his clothing.

1) The signs of infection.—They were "greenish or reddish" spots in garments of wool, linen, and leather. The plague was like unto mold

or mildew which commonly results from dampness, want of air and light. God speaks of it as leprosy. As this disease gradually destroys human life, so in clothing it frets away the strength and substance.

The signs of infection in man's social garments are unmistakably plain. They are manifest: (*a*) In the home. It was founded in divine wisdom (Gen. 2:18-24), but is spotted by divorce "for every cause," whereas Jesus said "except for fornication" (Matt. 19:3-9). (*b*) In the state. Civil government was "ordained of God" for man's "good" and for a restraint on "him that is evil" (Rom. 13:1-7), but it is infected by greed, tyranny and political corruption. (*c*) In business. Trading and getting gain are divinely encouraged (Jas. 4:13-15; cp. Matt. 25:14-30), but commerce has a code of its own in which, in many cases, honesty is set down at a heavy discount. (*d*) In education. Schools, books, and literature are indispensable means of human progress, but these also have a fretting leprosy. In the classroom the God of the Bible, in whom is all wisdom (Job 28: 12, 23), is replaced by the god of the human concept. The student is directed to feed his intellect on wisdom emitted by drunken poets of the past and infidel writers of modern times, while the divinely given textbook for the human race is entirely ignored. Pagan morality is often glorified at the expense of Christian ethics. (*e*) In amusement. Man's capacity for amusement demands amusement. But amusement must be recreative, not destructive. Man is a complex being of spirit, soul and body (1 Thess. 5:23) and anything which harms these parts is illegal. Modern amusements, particularly the movies and the dance, with their low ideals and sexual appeal, do not build up but destroy. (f) In religion. The church was intended by her Lord to be "the pillar and ground of the truth" (1 Tim. 3:15). To this end she was to be united in faith, clean in life and aggressive in action. But instead of unity there is division; her garments of holiness are spotted by the world; her program of progress is hampered by human devices in message and methods.

2) The method of procedure.

(a) All the people on watch.—Every article of clothing, or piece of fabric, or skin of animals, was liable at any time to become infected by the plague. Without delay it must be showed unto the priest. Individual responsibility of being continually on the lookout was levied upon every Israelite.

Personal responsibility is one obligation in the church of Christ. The Christian is commanded to "watch" his conduct (Mark 13:33-37), to "mark" the schismatic in the church (Rom. 16:17, 18), to "beware" of false teachers (Matt. 7:15). Like Paul, he is "set for the defense of the gospel" (Phil. 1:16).

(b) Inspection by the priest.—The record says it "shall be showed unto the priest. And the priest shall look on the plague." He was to judge the matter according to the divine law, and his decision was final.

In dealing with matters of our environment things arise which baffle human judgment. Jesus, our priest, whose eyes are "like a flame of fire" (Rev. 2:18), is the only one competent to diagnose the case and to solve all our problems. God has "spoken unto us in his Son." True, he is personally in heaven, but his word is with us. It is "quick to discern" and final in authority (Heb. 4:12; 2 Tim. 3:16, 17).

(c) Treatment of garments.

(1) "Burn."—If the plague, after a period of seven days, be spread in warp, or woof, or in the skin; or if it be not spread but its color remains unchanged, the priest "shall burn the garment." The law had no provision for its restoration.

(2) "Wash."—After seven days, if the plague is not spread, "then the priest shall command that they wash the thing." And if the plague departs, "then it shall be washed a second time, and shall be clean."

The application of this treatment to social disorders is obvious. There are some things so badly diseased that they never can be cured. Such is the condition of political governments, hence the heavenly Priest has declared that they shall be burned—removed (Rev. 16:18-20; cp. 11:15). What hope is there of reforming some popular amusements? Take, for instance, the movies. They are founded in greed and erected in sensuality. Washing will not do them any good. And what can be done with the saloon? It stands condemned before God and men. The effect of its goods and the atmosphere of its habitation are only evil continually. There is no reform for that establishment. Its place is in the everlasting burnings. What possibility is there of reforming the apostate church? It has been tried for centuries without avail. The Scriptures speak of it as "the man of sin," "the beast" and "the great harlot." God himself has abandoned all hope of her recovery and has decreed that she must be burned (Rev. 18).

Other articles there are in our social fabric which are less malignant. By thorough washing the plague in them can be removed. In the New Testament this washing is called "the washing of regeneration" (Titus 3:5). This type of reform is individual and begins within. It results in "a new creature," or creation (2 Cor. 5:17; cp. Eph. 4:24), which in turn will produce a new social order. It is the only divine program for the renovation of human society.

c) Leprosy of houses, Leviticus 14:33-57.

This leprosy was not traceable to natural causes, but sent of Jehovah. He said to Moses and Aaron,

"I put the plague of leprosy in a house." As a type it teaches that man's dwelling place, the earth, is affected by sin. Because of the transgression by Adam and Eve Jehovah said "cursed is the ground" (Gen. 3:17, 18). "The creation was subjected to vanity . . . and travaileth in pain" (Rom. 8:20, 22; cp. Isa. 24:5). Thorns, thistles, pests, storms, floods, earthquakes, deserts are so many evidences of the fact of sin.

1) The treatment of the plague.—The owner reported the infection to the priest who commanded the house to be emptied. If "greenish or reddish" depressions appeared in the wall, the house was shut up seven days for observation. Then: (*a*) If curable, the affected stones and all the plaster were replaced by new material. (*b*) If incurable, the house was torn down and carried out of the city into an unclean place.

The type presents two facts about the physical creation. (*a*) Some of it will be destroyed. "The earth and the works that are therein shall be burned up" (2 Pet. 3:10). The present constitution of nature and also the works of man bear the marks of sin, but these will finally be erased. The antediluvian world was purified by water; the present creation will be cleansed by fire. (*b*) Some of it will be reconstructed. The Bible begins with the generations of the heavens and the earth; it ends with their regeneration. This is made certain by such words as "perish," "changed," "dissolved"

(Heb. 1:11, 12; 2 Pet. 3:12). From these words we are not to understand that this physical universe will be annihilated, but recreated.

The purpose in the change is: (*a*) To forget "the former things" (Isa. 65:17). The ravages of sin are not pleasant to contemplate, therefore they are to be completely obliterated. (*b*) To make it a fit place for the new Jerusalem (Rev. 21:1, 2). The present world was created to meet the needs of the mortal body; the new world will be adapted to the immortal body.

2) The atonement for the house.—If the plague was healed the priest took two birds, one of which he killed over a vessel of running water. In this mixture he dipped the living bird and cedar wood, scarlet and hyssop, and sprinkled the house seven times, after which the living bird was let go: "So shall he make atonement for the house; and it shall be clean."

Here is a material house atoned for by water and blood. What the typical teaching? Plainly this, that man's redemption by the blood of Christ is not complete apart from a redeemed earth as his future dwelling place. Christ has sanctified this earth by his visit to it, by his blood falling upon it, by his people being buried in it and by his purpose of renovating it for man's eternal abode. And now the creation is waiting in hope to "be delivered from the bondage of corruption into the liberty of the glory of the children of God" (Rom. 8:20, 21).

From this concrete and illustrative teaching on sin certain truths are outstanding.

First, sin is a terrible fact. We have seen that it is morally unclean, hereditary, transmissible, and a living death; even nature itself is made to feel its blighting effect. The modern idea that sin is merely a failure of the individual to rise to the best that is in him is not in harmony with all this teaching of Jehovah on the nature and effect of sin.

Second, the cure of sin is a glorious reality. It is effected by divine power through the means of blood and water. In the language of divine revelation, the sinner is "cleansed" of his pollution, "atonement" is provided for him, and "creation itself shall be delivered from the bondage of corruption." It means that sin and its effect will finally be eradicated from the universe, and holiness shall once more characterize the whole creation of God.

XVI

HOLY SEASONS

In the Jewish economy there were weekly, monthly, and yearly days of worship. These "set feasts of Jehovah" were "holy convocations" designed: (1) To furnish occasion for moral and spiritual improvement. (2) To keep alive the memory of past events. (3) To serve as prophetic types of the good things to come.

1. *The Sabbath,* Leviticus 23:1-3—

The name of this seventh day of the Hebrew week means "rest." It was founded on the needs of the human constitution, providing rest for the body and worship for the spirit. Man is like a seven-day clock that runs down and needs to be rewound.

a) Observance—

1) In the home. No work must be done (Exod. 20:10); nor fire kindled (Exod. 35:3). The penalty was death (Exod. 31:14, 15).

2) In the sanctuary. The daily sacrifices were doubled (Exod. 29:38-41; Num. 28:9, 10); the show-bread was replaced (Lev. 24:5-8); the Scriptures were read (Luke 4:16, 17; Acts 13:27).

b) Design—

1) It was a day of rest, worship, and rejoicing (Exod. 20:10; Isa. 58:13, 14).

2) It was commemorative:

(*a*) Of the creation of the world (Exod. 20:11).

(*b*) Of Israel's bondage in Egypt and deliverance (Deut. 5:15). This made the day Jewish and it was intended for the Jews only.

3) It was a sign between Jehovah and Israel (Exod. 31:13, 16, 17). As such it reminded them of their covenant relation to Jehovah.

c) Type—

As a day of rest it was "a shadow of the things to come" (Col. 2:16, 17).

1) Of rest in Christ here (Matt. 11:28, 29). That is obtained through forgiveness of sin (Mark 16:16; Acts 2:38) and results in a peace which the world cannot give (John 14:27; 16:33). It is a soul rest.

2) Of rest through Christ hereafter. As "God rested on the seventh day from all his works," so "there remaineth (in the future) a sabbath rest for the people of God" (Heb. 4:4, 9, 10). It is the heavenly rest from labors of earth occasioned by sin (Rev. 14:13).

2. *The Passover*—

This was one of three yearly festivals which every male Israelite was commanded to attend (Deut. 16:16).

The Hebrew word for "Passover" is derived from a root which means to "leap over," "to spare," "to show mercy," hence a sacrifice of mercy (cp. Exod. 12:12, 13). The purpose in this feast as a type is to show how God in mercy spares the life of the sinner through Jesus Christ (1 Cor. 5:7; Titus 3:5).

In the law governing this feast, as given in Exodus 12, the following facts are noted:

a) The time.—The calendar was changed (vs. 2). Abib or Nisan, the seventh month of the civil year, became the first month of the sacred year. Hence the distinction among the Jews between the sacred and civil year began with the first Passover.

In the antitype also there was a change of the calendar from A.U.C., the year the city of Rome was founded, to A.D., the year of the Lord's birth. Moreover, the day of rest was changed from the seventh of the week to the first.

b) The victim.—Several important matters were observed.

1) It was without blemish (vs. 5). For the purpose of observation in regard to this matter, the lamb was taken on the tenth day and kept till the fourteenth. For three and a half years Christ was publicly observed by men, and his record reads, "a lamb without blemish and without spot" (1 Pet. 1:19).

2) It was to be a matured male a year old from the sheep or the goats (vs. 5). Christ was a male who had reached maturity at the time of his death, thus giving himself in the full strength of manhood.

3) It was killed at even on the fourteenth, about three o'clock (vs. 6), the time Israel came out of Egypt (Deut. 16:6). At the same time, when the daily evening sacrifice of a lamb took place in Jerusalem, the Lamb of God expired on the cross (Matt. 27:45-50).

4) Its blood was sprinkled on the lintel and the two side-posts of the door, thus Israel was saved by the blood of the lamb (vs. 22). By the same token the life of the sinner is spared by the blood of the Lamb of God, when it is applied (John 1:29).

5) It was roasted whole, not a bone was broken (vss. 9, 46). When the Roman soldiers came to Jesus they did not break his bones that this Scripture might be fulfilled (John 19:36). And the spiritual body of Christ, the church, must not be dismembered or broken by divisions (1 Cor. 10:16, 17).

6) Its remains which were not eaten were burned (vs. 10). None of it must remain until morning. This was done to keep it from corruption. Accordingly Christ was raised on the third day and his body did not see corruption (Luke 24:1-7; Acts 2:24-28).

c) The eating—

1) They were to eat it in that night (vs. 8). Since the lamb was killed in the afternoon of the fourteenth, the night referred to would fall on the fifteenth, for the Jewish day began and ended

at sunset. In like manner Christ's sacrifice benefits nobody unless appropriated by faith and obedience (John 6:35, 51-58).

2) They were to eat it as ready for the journey (vs. 11). Canaan, not Egypt, was to be their future home, hence they must consider themselves as pilgrims. Such is the condition of mankind now. All are on the way, but do they know where they are going? God's people in particular are addressed as "sojourners and pilgrims" (1 Pet. 2:11; Luke 12:35), for they are on the way to the heavenly Canaan.

3) They were to eat it in haste (vs. 11). Because of the menace of the enemy and because of the impending divine judgment upon the Egyptians, the Israelites had no time to lose. The appeal of the gospel to men reads, "now is the day of salvation" (2 Cor. 6:2). The refusal brings "eternal destruction from the face of the Lord" (1 Thess. 1:7-9).

4) They were to eat it without leaven (vs. 8). The unleavened bread was called "the bread of affliction" (Deut. 16:3), and as a symbol it stood for the old life of bondage. When one becomes a Christian, he resolutely separates himself from the old life of sin (Rom. 6:1-4; 1 Thess. 5:22).

5) They were to eat it with bitter herbs (vs. 8). This would remind them of their bitter experience in Egypt (cp. Exod. 1:11, 13, 14). Such

is the experience of the slave of sin. It is a hard life which terminates in death. (Prov. 13:15; Rom. 6:23).

6) They were to eat it as a memorial (vs. 14). In partaking of the lamb, they were to remember the day when they came out of Egypt (Deut. 16:3). A like provision is made for the Christian in the Lord's Supper. It is a memorial of his deliverance from the power of darkness through the death of Christ (Luke 22:19, 20).

d) The feast of unleavened bread (vss. 15-20).—This commenced with the eating of the Passover and lasted for seven days. Like the Passover lamb, it was to recall their experience in Egypt, with this difference: The slain lamb spared their lives; the unleavened bread indicated separation from Egypt, for they left in such haste as not to have time for leavening their bread.

To this part of the type Paul refers when he says to the Christian, "Purge out the old leaven" and "let us keep the feast" (1 Cor. 5:7, 8). And as the feast of unleavened bread was kept for seven days, a complete period of time, so God's people are to serve him in righteousness and holiness all the days of their life.

e) The sheaf of the first-fruits, Leviticus 23:9-14. On the morrow after the Passover Sabbath, the third day after killing the Passover lamb, a sheaf of the first fruits of the barley harvest was presented as a wave offering before Jehovah. In addition there were offered a he-lamb a year old, some fine flour, oil and wine.

The typical import of this wave offering is seen in the resurrection of Christ. As in the type, he arose on the third day which was also the first day of the week. Accordingly Paul speaks of him as "the firstfruits of them that are asleep." And as the first fruits of the type sanctified the rest of the harvest, so mankind has been set apart for resurrection from the grave by the resurrection of Christ (1 Cor. 15:20, 22).

3. *The Feast of Weeks*—

This festival which lasted one day, was known by three Old Testament names: "The feast of weeks" (Deut. 16:9-12), because it came seven weeks after the Passover Sabbath; "the feast of harvest" (Exod. 23:16), because it came at the close of the wheat harvest; "the day of the firstfruits" (Num. 28:26), because the first fruits of the harvest were offered to Jehovah. Its New Testament name is Pentecost (Acts 2:1), a Greek name meaning fiftieth, because the festival came on the fiftieth day after the Passover Sabbath (Lev. 23:15, 16).

a) The observance of the day.—All ablebodied males were to attend, each to bring an offering according to his ability (Deut. 16:16, 17). Besides the regular daily offerings, the festive sacrifices for the day, according to Numbers 28:26-31, were two young bullocks, one ram, seven he-lambs a year old for a burnt offering along with their meal offering, and one he-goat for a sin offering.

Then came the peculiar offering described in Leviticus 23:17-20 which gave the day its distinctive significance. It consisted of two loaves of bread made of flour from the first fruits of the wheat harvest and baked with leaven. Their accompanying sacrifices were for a burnt offering, seven lambs a year old, one young bullock, two rams with meal offering and drink offerings; for a sin offering, one he-goat; for a peace offering, two lambs a year old, the same with the two loaves to be waved before Jehovah as a public peace and thank offering of all Israel.

Lastly, the people presented their own freewill offerings, according as Jehovah had prospered them, the same to be partaken of as a festive meal to which the stranger, the poor and the Levites were invited. It was a day of rejoicing before Jehovah because of liberation from Egyptian bondage (Deut. 16:11, 12).

b) The typical teaching—

1) The significance of time.—It is calculated from Exodus 19 that the Law was given on Mount Sinai fifty days after the first Passover in Egypt. The usual way of counting these fifty days is: The Passover lamb was killed on the fourteenth day of the first month, which leaves seventeen days, including the fourteenth; thirty days in the second

month; Israel arrived at Sinai "In the third month," possibly on the first day, though we are not positively told; and after two days of preparing the people, Jehovah descended and gave the law to Moses thus making in all fifty days. Accordingly Jewish tradition at the time of Christ held that the Day of Pentecost was the anniversary of the giving of the law. Therefore, the beginning of the Jewish religion was on the first Pentecost, while the commencement of the Christian religion was certainly on the last Pentecost when the new and better law was given on Mount Zion in Jerusalem.

Moreover, since the count of time for the Feast of Weeks began and ended on the day after the weekly Sabbath (Lev. 23:15, 16), so the day of the last Pentecost came on the first day of the week. Like the day of the type, it was divinely set apart for "a holy convocation" of the Lord's people in memory of his resurrection from the grave.

2) The meaning of offerings.—The two kinds of offerings in the type, the bloody and the bloodless, were fulfilled on the day of Pentecost.

First, the bloody offerings of bullocks, sheep and goats were answered to by the preaching of the day. The gospel facts proclaimed proved that Jesus died for our sins; that he was buried; that he was raised from the dead; and that he ascended into heaven where he was crowned both Lord and Christ.

Second, the wave offering of the first fruits had its counterpart in the converts on Pentecost. On that day not less than three thousand, called "the first fruits" (Rom. 11:16), were presented as a wave offering unto the Lord of glory. It is not without significance that on the day Moses descended from the Mount with the Law, three thousand Israelites were slain with the sword (Exod. 32), and when the Holy Spirit descended with the new law three thousand Israelites were slain by the sword of the Spirit and were made alive unto God.

Lastly, in the type there was manifest the spirit of brotherhood and happiness as each shared with the other in festal eating and all rejoiced before Jehovah. Likewise those on Pentecost who heard, believed and obeyed the gospel "had all things common," and "they took their food with gladness and singleness of heart, praising God."

4. *The Feast of Trumpets—*

Directions for making and using the trumpets are given in Numbers 10:1-10. It will be observed that they were the voice of Jehovah summoning his people to worship, to journeying, to war; they sounded at the set feasts; they ushered in every month of the year; they were blown over some of the sacrifices. The end in view with reference to Israel was twofold: "Ye shall be remembered before Jehovah"; in turn they should remember him, "I am Jehovah your God." Thus the sound of the trumpet established a mutual relationship between Jehovah and his people.

But there was a special significance attached to its use on the first day of the seventh month, Tishri, and for two reasons: First, it being the seventh, it was the sabbatical month in which occurred the great feasts Atonement and Tabernacles. Second, this month marked the beginning of the civil year, hence its celebration was a new-year festival.

a) The observance of the type.—According to directions for the day in Numbers 29: 1-6, there was a holy convocation when the trumpets were sounded continually from morning till evening, "a day of blowing of trumpets." Besides the daily offerings, there were the ordinary new moon sacrifices prescribed in Numbers 28:11-15 by which each month was consecrated to Jehovah. Following these the special offerings on this day were for a burnt offering, one young bullock, one ram, seven he-lambs a year old without blemish, with their appropriate meal and drink offerings; one he-goat for a sin offering. The whole was regarded as "a memorial before God" (Num. 10:10) and as "a sweet savor" into him.

b) The teaching of the antitype.—As indicated above, the blowing of the trumpet was a symbol of God's voice which directed the movements of his people and called them to worship. As an ordinance it looked forward to the Christian age when the gospel trumpet should summon "all flesh to worship before Jehovah" in the spiritual temple, the church (Isa. 66:23; Ezek. 46:1). It was therefore a type of the preaching of the gospel. And the blowing of the gospel trumpet is not to be in an "uncertain voice" (1 Cor. 14:8; cp. Gal. 1:8, 9).

The first peal of this trumpet was heard in Jerusalem on the day of Pentecost in A.D. 34. From that place its joyful sound went forth in every direction until it was heard "in all creation under heaven" (Col. 1:23). This will continue until Christ is proclaimed and acclaimed king universal (Rev. 11:15; cp. Ps. 72:11). And finally, as in the type Jehovah's people were summoned by the trumpet, so in the day of Christ's second coming, "them that are fallen asleep in Jesus" shall be awakened "with the trump of God" (1 Thes. 4:13-18) and "shall gather together from the four winds, from one end of heaven to the other" (Matt. 24:31).

5. *The Day of Atonement—*

The name "atonement," from the Hebrew *kaphar*, means to cover, the object being to put out of sight the sins of the nation of Israel for a whole year. This most impressive day in the Jewish calendar came on the tenth of the seventh month, Tishri. It was "a sabbath of solemn rest" in which the people were to "afflict their souls" by penitence and fasting (cp. Ps. 35:13).

The law for observing the day is found in Leviticus 16:1-34; Numbers 29:7-11.

a) The order of services.—From Numbers 29:7-11 the offerings seem to have been three kinds: First, "the continual burnt offering" which was offered daily morning and evening; next the festive sacrifices of the day, the burnt offering consisting of one young bullock, one ram, seven he-lambs a year old, with meal offerings of fine flour mingled with oil; and, third, "the sin offering of atonement," the one with special meaning for the day, was a young bullock for the high priest and his house, and two goats for the people.

The work of the high priest in relation to the atonement offerings is of chief interest. In Leviticus 16 definite directions are given for his procedure. It was the only day in the year on which he was allowed to go into the Most Holy Place of the tabernacle. He was robed in his white garments, symbolic of that purity sought by the offerings. And because these were "the holy garments," he must bathe his whole body before he put them on.

On this day he labored alone to utter exhaustion in presenting the three kinds of offerings. To accomplish atonement, first, he killed the bullock for himself and family, after which he took the blood into the Holy of Holies where it was sprinkled seven times on and before the mercy seat of the ark while incense was burning. Next, he designated by lot each of the two goats, one for sacrifice and one for removal. Having killed the goat for the people, he took its blood into the Holy of Holies and sprinkled it seven times on and before the mercy seat. Then, on account of "the uncleanness of the children of Israel and all their sins," he made atonement for the Holy Place by sprinkling the blood of the bullock and the goat upon the altar of incense seven times, and upon the tent of meeting, the priests, and all the people. As a final act, the high priest laid both his hands upon the head of the live goat, confessed the iniquities of the people, and sent him away into the wilderness.

b) The typical significance—

1) The time.—As Jehovah set the time for the type, so He did for the antitype. Christ appeared in "the fulness of the time" (Gal. 4:4, 5). And as the day of atonement occurred but once a year, a complete revolution of time, so Christ has been "once offered to bear the sins of many," hence "there remaineth no more a sacrifice for sins" (Heb. 9:28; 10:26). The day of his crucifixion, therefore, was the day of all days in this world year.

2) The high priest—

(*a*) His dress.—As his white garments, symbolic of purity, were essential in order to secure atonement, so the Savior of the world must be, and he was, "without sin" (Heb. 4:15). For this reason he could become "unto all them that obey him the author of eternal salvation" (Heb. 5:9).

(b) His labors.—On that day he labored alone. "There shall be no man in the tent of meeting when he goeth in to make atonement." Thus it was with our High Priest when he accomplished atonement for the sins of the world. "His own self bare our sins in his body upon the tree" (1 Pet. 2:24). Even God himself forsook him (Matt. 27:46). He suffered, bled and died alone!

And as the labors of the high priest brought utter exhaustion, so that at the close, we are told, the people extended him sympathetic congratulation on having been able to finish, so our Lord bore the exhausting sin-load of the world. Its burden he felt in the garden (Luke 22:41-44), on the cross (Isa. 53:6), and at last he "yielded up his spirit" (Matt. 27:50).

3) The atonement—

(a) Inability of the type.—"The law made nothing perfect." This appeared, first, in the imperfect high priest who "offered up sacrifices, first for his own sins, and then for the sins of the people" (Heb. 7:27); and, second, in the imperfect atonement, "for it is impossible that the blood of bulls and goats should take away sins" (Heb. 10:4). Therefore, there was need of "a new covenant" and "a death for the transgressions under the first covenant" (Heb. 9:15).

(*b*) The victims.—They were divinely selected through the law of Jehovah, a bullock for the priests and two goats for the people. The peculiar method of selecting the goats was as follows: Two pieces of wood, or stone, or mettle were put in a vessel. On one piece was written "for Jehovah," on the other "for Azazel." After having shaken the vessel the high priest took one lot in each hand and laid one on the head of each goat. The one for Jehovah was slain, the one for Azazel was sent away alive into the wilderness. The Scriptures tell us that Jehovah disposed of the lots (Prov. 16:33). Similarly, when in divine Providence it became necessary to select the victim for the world's guilt, Christ was the chosen of God (Isa. 42:1; Acts 2:23).

(*c*) Necessity of blood.—"All things are cleansed with blood" (Heb. 9:22). For that reason the blood of these victims, when applied, ceremonially cleansed the worshiper and restored communion with God. But these sacrifices could not, "as touching the conscience, make the worshipper perfect," therefore, it took the blood of Christ "to cleanse your conscience from dead works to serve the living God" (Heb. 9:9, 14).

(*d*) Entering the Most Holy Place.—The high priest, after having killed the sacrifices, entered the Most Holy Place with the blood which he sprinkled "for himself and for the errors of the people" (Heb. 9:7). In like manner, Christ "through his own blood entered into heaven itself, now to appear before the face of God for us" (Heb. 9:12, 24). And as the priest sprinkled the blood with reference to sin, so Christ applies his blood in heaven to the sinner when he hears, believes and obeys the gospel.

Not only was blood presented in the Most Holy Place, but incense also was offered. Incense was a type of prayer (Rev. 5:8), and accordingly it is said of Christ that "he ever liveth to make intercession for them who draw near to God through him" (Heb. 7:25).

(e) The live goat.—The final act in the atonement ceremony, a rite strange and mysterious, was the disposal of the live goat. Aaron laid both his hands upon its head and confessed over it all the iniquities of the children of Israel. Having thus symbolically loaded it with the sins of the people, it was led away out of sight into the wilderness. There is but one meaning that can be given to this climactic part of the type. The slain goat typified the means of atonement, the live one its effect. It tells the story that when sins have been atoned for by the blood of Christ, they are out of sight for ever. The new covenant reads, "Their sins will I remember no more" (Heb. 8:12). He will "cast all of their sins into the depths of the sea" (Micah 7:19). "As far as the east is from the west, so far hath he removed our transgressions from us" (Ps. 103:12). Atonement means to cover!

6. *The Feast of Tabernacles*—

This was the third annual festival which all males must attend. It began on the fifteenth of the seventh month, Tishri, lasted seven days, and was followed by one day of holy convocation. According to its name, the people dwelt in booths to commemorate the tent life in the journey from Egypt to Canaan (Lev. 23:43). It was also called "the feast of ingathering" (Exod. 23:16), because it came after the harvest and vintage.

a) Characteristics of the feast—

1) Its joyous festivities, Deuteronomy 16:13-15.—"Thou shalt rejoice . . . and thou shalt be altogether joyful." All Hebrew festivals were seasons of rejoicing before Jehovah, but this feast excelled them all. This was a natural consequent of the abundant ingathering with which Jehovah had blessed them in that goodly land. The expression of this joy was provided for in a great seven-day banquet to which every man contributed according to the measure he had been blessed of Jehovah. To this feast were invited the poor, the rich, the servant, the sojourner, the fatherless and the widow as welcome guests in the name of Jehovah.

2) The dwelling in booths.—According to the law, the booths were constructed of "branches of palm-trees, and boughs of thick trees, and willows of the brook" (Lev. 23:40; cp. Neh. 8:15). The design was, "that your generation may know

that I made the children of Israel dwell in booths, when I brought them out of the land of Egypt."

3) The sacrifices, Numbers 29:12-38.—Besides the regular morning and evening sacrifices, for each day there was a burnt offering of two rams, fourteen he-lambs with their meal and drink offerings; one he-goat for a sin offering. But what was most peculiar was the daily sacrifice of bullocks. They decreased every day by one from thirteen on the first day to seven on the last day. The eighth day, like the first, called for a solemn assembly and no servile work. The burnt offering was one bullock, one ram, seven lambs, with their appropriate meal and drink offerings; one he-goat for a sin offering. For the seven days there were sacrificed 70 bullocks, 14 rams, 98 lambs, and 7 goats in order to keep before the people that sin has death in it, and that redemption therefrom requires blood.

b) The type in fulfillment.—From the two prominent ideas associated with the feast of tabernacles, the forty years of tent life and gratitude for harvest, the typical teaching must include some things in the Christian's career between his deliverance from spiritual bondage and his entrance into the eternal rest of which Canaan was a type.

1) The tent life.—As pilgrims in the journey to the heavenly country, we are now living in a tent. "For we know that if the earthly house of our tabernacle (literally, our earthly house which is a tent) be dissolved, we have a building

from God" (2 Cor. 5:1). As the booths were Israel's temporary dwellings for seven days, a full period of time, so our bodies are the temporary dwellings of our spirits during our earthly stay. And as the booths in the type were taken down at the end of the week and the Israelites moved into permanent homes, so our present tent-house shall be dissolved at the end of our earthly week and we shall move into the permanent dwelling of the resurrection body.

2) The rejoicing.—To Israel the reasons for rejoicing were two: First, the historical, deliverance from bondage (Lev. 23:43); second, the agricultural, harvest from the land flowing with milk and honey. For similar reasons the Christian's life is to be characterized by gratitude. His deliverance from the slavery of sin into fellowship with God, and his daily enjoyment of material blessings from his Father's bounty are sufficient reasons for the apostolic admonition, "Rejoice in the Lord always: again I will say, Rejoice" (Phil. 4:4). And as in the type Jehovah provided for the expression of joy in a common meal to which all contributed according to blessings bestowed, so God has arranged for the Christian to share with the needy world material and spiritual blessings "as he may prosper" (1 Cor. 16:2; Rom. 12:13, 20). This sharing is a direct outflow of "abundance of joy," divinely motivated and approved, for "God loveth a cheerful giver" (2 Cor. 8:2; 9:7).

The presence and words of Jesus at the feast of Tabernacles in Jerusalem are important (John 7:37, 38). It was on the eighth day, "the great day of the feast," that he "stood and cried, saying, If any man thirst, let him come unto me and drink." On that last day of unbounded joy he offered himself to the world as its spiritual sustenance and everlasting joy.

The typical significance of sacred time is impressively presented in the divine treatise we have considered. Through the use of the calendar Jehovah prepared for us a series of lessons on atonement for sin, the beginning of the gospel age, the tent life of our sojourn here, the resurrection from the grave and the heavenly rest. By the same means he trained his people of that day through moral and spiritual culture resulting from careful observance of the type.

The effect may be better understood from a summary of the time they devoted for this purpose. In the Jewish sacred year there were 52 Sabbaths, 12 New Moon festivals, 8 days for Passover and Unleavened Bread, 1 day for Feast of Weeks, 1 day for Feast of Trumpets, 1 day for Atonement, 7 days for Feast of Tabernacles, 30 days for morning and evening sacrifices (2 hours daily), an average of 52 days for each year from the sabbatical year, and an average of seven days for each year from the year of Jubilee—a total of 171 days. Add to this the feasts not commanded by Jehovah, such as Purim, Dedication, Wood-Carrying, etc.;

the time for going and coming to and from the festivals; the time spent for private and personal devotion (Deut. 6:4-9), and it will be found that fully one-half of the year was devoted by the Jew to religious and moral improvement. This fact should serve as a distinct rebuke to the present generation who in effect say, "We have not time to be religious."

XVII

THE TABERNACLE

There was no divinely ordained house of prayer, no tabernacle of worship on this earth from Adam to Moses. The first religious institution was the altar, the second the tabernacle, the third the church. The tabernacle was designed as a type and illustration of the entire Christian institution (Heb. 9:8, 9), therefore knowledge of its structure and typology is indispensable to a clear understanding of the gospel. It was not a copy of anything existing on earth, but of heavenly things (Heb. 9:23). On Mount Sinai Jehovah gave Moses the pattern, commanded him to build, and later inspired the workmen for the task. When construction was finished the God of Israel took up his residence in the tent for the purpose of dwelling among his people.

1. *Names*—

Jehovah not only builds religious institutions, but he also names them.

a) The "tent" (Exod. 26:36), because Jehovah would dwell in it (Exod. 25:8). When man had sinned, God did not abandon him but dwelt along the side of him in the tabernacle and the temple. Now he dwells in the church through the Holy Spirit.

b) "The tent of meeting" (Exod. 27:21), because there Jehovah would meet with his people. Fellowship with God is the core of religion, hence Christians are in fellowship with divine personalities (1 John 1:3; 2 Cor. 13:14).

c) "The tabernacle of the testimony" (Num. 1:50), because (*a*) the ark in it contained the two tables of stone called "the testimony," (*b*) from the ark Jehovah spoke to the people (Exod. 25:21, 22). After the same likeness the church is the place of divine revelation, for to her was given the word of God (1 Cor. 2:9, 10, 13).

d) "The house of Jehovah" (Deut. 23:18), because it belonged to him, hence it must be approached in reverence and handled with care. Analogous to this Christ has now a house, "whose house are we," "bought with a price" (Heb. 3:6; 1 Cor. 6:20).

e) "A sanctuary" (Exod. 25:8), because it was a holy place. Therefore holiness must characterize the worshipers. For the same reason God's people are now commanded to be holy (1 Pet. 1:15).

f) "The temple of Jehovah" (1 Sam. 1:9), because it was the place where he was worshiped. There only he recorded his name and met with his people. The church is now the "temple of God" (1 Cor. 3:16). It is the only institution on earth in which his name is recorded, and there only can Christ be approached and glorified (Eph. 3:21).

2. *History*—

a) The date.—The tabernacle was set up on the first day of the first month in the sacred year which began a new count of time (Exod. 40:1, 2). It was the day of Israel's redemption from slavery in Egypt (Exod. 12:2, 41, 42), and also the beginning of a new religious institution.

It is significant that the antitype, the church, a new religious institution, was founded on the Day of Pentecost, on the first day of the week, which was also a new count of time in memory of Christ's resurrection. It was the day of man's liberation from the bondage of sin, for then the shackles were struck from three thousand slaves.

b) The model.—Jehovah was the architect who drew the pattern for Moses to follow (Exod. 25:9, 40). This he also did for the temple of Solomon (1 Chron. 28:19). It is to be marked that Jehovah has never allowed man to originate a single religious institution.

Like the tabernacle the church was built according to a divine model (Matt. 16:18). For that reason it is called "the church of God" (1 Cor. 1:2), because he planned it and Christ executed the plan through his apostles. Thus in type and antitype God gave the patterns and was the builder through chosen persons. In these matters men have infringed on divine rights, hence the different kinds of churches now in existence. This church confusion can be corrected only by going back to the divine model.

c) The material.—It was in the nature of a freewill offering from the people of things they had asked from the Egyptians and which were due for service rendered (Exod. 25:1-9; cp. 12:35, 36). Thus they co-operated with Jehovah in this important building enterprise. In gratitude for deliverance from bondage the Hebrews brought more than was needed and a proclamation was issued to restrain them (Exod. 36:5-7). The tabernacle with furnishings cost about $1,500,000.

In like manner when the church was established, there was divine and human co-operation. Christ by the Holy Spirit in Peter announced the plan of salvation, then he called upon the hearers to save themselves through obedience, and as many as "received his word were baptized" (Acts 2:38, 40, 41). In gratitude for divine mercy extended to them, three thousand answered the call and gave themselves willingly as building material for the "spiritual house" (1 Pet. 2:5).

d) The workmen.—They were divinely selected and inspired for the work (Exod. 31:1-11; 35:30—36:2). Moses directed the construction through two foremen, Bezalel and Oholiab, "filled with the Spirit of God," who were over "every wise-hearted man, in whose heart Jehovah had put wisdom." No mistake must be made, because the structure was to be an exact "copy of heavenly things" (Heb. 8:5).

In the same way the New Testament church was built. Jesus selected his apostles and qualified them for the work by inspiration of the Holy Spirit (John 16:13; Acts 2:4). The inspiration of the workers enabled them to construct the spiritual house in harmony with the type and to give to the world a perfect institution for worship.

e) The cloud.—When Moses had finished the work, "the cloud covered the tent of meeting, and the glory of Jehovah filled the tabernacle" (Exod. 40:34-38). Thus Jehovah took up his residence in the sanctuary and traveled with his people. By night the cloud became luminous so as to give light to the camp. By day it was a shade from the scorching sun (cp. Ps. 105:39). It also served as a guide in the way from Egypt to Canaan (Exod. 13:21, 22).

On the Day of Pentecost when the spiritual house was erected, there was also a miraculous demonstration of divine presence. Then Jehovah took up his residence in the church through the Holy Spirit (Acts 2:38; cp. 1 Cor. 3:16). No longer does he dwell along the side of man, as in the tabernacle and temple, but in him as in the beginning before sin caused separation. His good Spirit is the light, comfort, and guide for the church in her earthly pilgrimage.

SHADOW AND SUBSTANCE   163

f) The location.—The outer court and the tent faced the East so that the people, when they came to worship, must turn their backs to the sun which they had worshiped in Egypt (cp. Ezek. 8:16). The position of the tabernacle in the camp was central in relation to the tribes and their leaders, so that it became the one object vision and interest to all the people. (See Num. 2, 3, and also diagram below.)

According to the type the church was intended to be the center of interest in human society. Like

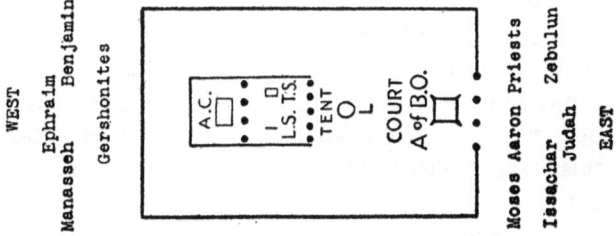

"a city set on a hill," it is seen by all and its glory should call forth the admiration of every beholder.

3. *Structure—*

In arrangement it was intended to illustrate the three states of man; Nature, Grace, and Glory.

a) The court, Exodus 27:9-19; 35:18.

2) Area.—The tent was set within a space 100 cubits long by 50 cubits wide, or 150 x 75 feet. This area was enclosed by a white linen curtain 5 cubits high, hung on 60 pillars, topped with silver, set in sockets of brass and held upright by cords and stakes. The entrance, 20 cubits wide, had a screen of fine linen embroidered in blue, purple, scarlet, and hung on 4 pillars.

This enclosure was a type of the world where Christ is preached. In Revelation 11:2 this court is occupied by "the nations," or the world to whom the gospel is proclaimed (Mark 16:15). This typical fact is further evident in that all Israelites could come into the court, but they did so as sinners with sacrifice asking for mercy. Man enters this state by fleshly birth and is dealt with as a sinner.

The white curtain was the first object seen by the Hebrews when they looked toward the tabernacle, and it conveyed the idea of purity and need of cleansing. The clean life of Christ has the same effect upon polluted man (Luke 5:8). The capitals, fillets and hooks on the pillars were made of the redemption silver given by the males from twenty years old and upward (Exod. 30:11-16; 38:25-31) which typified our redemption through Christ (1 Pet. 1:18, 19). The brass foundation for the pillars was symbolic of strength (Jer. 1:18), and was a type of Christ, the "sure foundation" for every believer (Isa. 28:16; cp. 1 Pet. 2:6). The veil, or screen, of variegated colors typified personal characteristics of Christ. The blue tells us he was from heaven, the purple indicates his royalty, the scarlet points to his sacrifice, the white speaks of his purity. The veil was hung on four pillars, typical of the four Gospels, for they contain the above facts concerning Christ and are designed to produce faith in him (John 20:31).

2) Contents.—Within this enclosure, besides the tent itself there were two objects illustrative of man's salvation from sin.

(*a*) The altar, Exodus 27:1-8.—Just inside the veil stood the altar of burnt offerings, 5 cubits square, 3 cubits high, made of acacia wood, overlaid with brass, the same metal being used for the ashpans, shovels, basins, fleshhooks, and fire pans which belonged to the altar. On top it had a horn at each corner to which the animals for sacrifice were bound (Ps. 118:27). It had two staves for carrying it when on march. The fire upon it, never to go out, was kindled by Jehovah (Lev. 6:13; 9:24). It was the great public altar on which were offered one lamb in the morning and one in the evening, with additional offerings on special occasions.

The New Testament tells us, "We have an altar," not a material one as in some churches, but "Jesus" (Heb. 13:10-12). He is also our sacrifice and priest. As the typical altar was seen through the veil, so we see Christ crucified through the four Gospels. Like the type, all men may come unto him for atonement for sin (John 12:32; 1 John 2:2).

(*b*) The laver, Exodus 38:8; 30:17-21.— This article was made from the mirrors of the women, and its place was between the altar and the tent. In it the priests were to bathe at consecration to office (Exod. 29:4) and before they entered the tent or officiated at the altar of burnt offerings. Neglect of this was punishable by death. It should be remembered that the common Jew could not go beyond the altar. From there on he was represented by the priest, therefore what the priest did in relation to the laver is additional illustration of what a sinner must do now to be saved.

As a type the laver had for its counterpart Christian baptism. By comparing the design of each this fact becomes clear.

First, there is cleansing.—As the Hebrew could not become a priest until he had been ceremonially cleansed by washing in the laver, so the sinner cannot become a priest of God until he has been cleansed "through the washing of regeneration" (Titus 3:5). In the margin the word for "washing" is "laver," *loutron*, which by metonomy stands for baptism. In the Greek translation of the Old Testament the same word for "laver" is found in Exodus 30:18. In Ephesians 5:26 the same word is used for cleansing the church, "having cleansed it by the washing (laver) of water with the word." To the same effect Hebrews 10:22 speaks of the body being "washed with pure water." From this it is seen that in baptism the sinner is regenerated, saved, cleansed, and purified. It is the consummating act in becoming a Christian.

Second, there is transition.—As washing in the laver was the condition on which to enter the tabernacle, a type of the church, so baptism is the means of entering the church of Christ. From the fact that the laver was made from the mirrors given by the women, it seems that Jesus used the word "see" in John 3:3, and in verse 5 he makes "water and Spirit" means of entering the kingdom. In Galatians 3:27 Paul speaks of baptism as the soul's journey into Christ. But this divine arrangement has been changed in modern teaching and practice. The laver has been moved from the court into the tabernacle; baptism has been made merely a church ordinance instead of an act of obedience "unto remission of sins" (Acts 2:38).

Finally, there is penalty.—Neglect of washing in the laver was punishable by death. That makes baptism of special importance. A greater penalty is affixed to the gospel. In 1 Peter 4:17 the question is asked, "What shall be the end of them that obey not the gospel of God?" The answer to that question is "eternal destruction from the face of the Lord" (2 Thess. 1:7-9). In the light of this penalty it is a serious matter to speak of baptism as "a non-essential."

b) The sanctuary, Exodus 26:1-25; 36:8-38.—The structure was 30 cubits long, 10 cubits wide, 10 cubits high, or 45 x 15 x 15 feet. It had two rooms, the first called the Holy Place was 20 cubits long; the second, the Most Holy Place was a perfect cube. In design it pictures the wonderful story of the church on earth and her relation to heaven.

1) Walls.

(*a*) Boards, Exodus 26:15-25.—In number they were 48, made of acacia wood and overlaid with gold. Of these 20 stood on each side and 8 on the west end. Each board was 10 cubits high by 1½ cubits broad.

Typically the boards represent the individual Christians who are spoken of as "living stones" in the spiritual house (1 Pet. 2-5). The gold speaks the preciousness of the church for which Christ gave his life (Eph. 5:25).

(b) Bars, Exodus 26:26-30.—The boards were held in place by five bars of acacia wood covered with gold. Four of these were on the outside and passed through gold rings fixed to each board, but the middle bar passed through the center of the boards (cp. Exod. 36:33).

Corresponding to these bars the church is held together by the authority of Christ (Col. 1:18), by the bond of love (Col. 3:14), by unity in Christ (1 Cor. 1:10), by the bond of peace (Eph. 4:3). As the middle bar passed through the boards, so God through the Holy Spirit is "through all, and in all" (Eph. 4:6).

(c) Foundation, Exodus 26:19-25.—At the lower end of each board were two tenons which were set in two silver blocks called sockets, made from the redemption money before mentioned. Each socket weighed a talent, or 93¾ lbs. (Exod. 38:27.)

This foundation of redemptive silver was a type of Christ our redemption upon whom the church is built (1 Cor. 3:11).

2) Roof, Exodus 26:1-14.—It had four covers. The first, or inner curtain, was of fine linen woven in blue, purple and scarlet, with figures of cherubim; the second was made of goat's hair, presumably white; the third was of rams' skins dyed red; the fourth was of sealskins. The material for the linen and goat's hair curtains was spun by the wise-hearted women and woven by the wise-hearted men (Exod. 35:25, 26; 36:8).

The roof with its four covers contained a revelation concerning Christ and the church. Beginning with the inside there was the rich tapestry of the linen curtain which covered the walls and formed the ceiling. The blue tells us that in the church we are "in the heavenly places, in Christ Jesus" (Eph. 2:6). The purple speaks of our royal dignity, for we are "a royal priesthood," "a kingdom of priests" (1 Pet. 2:9; Rev. 1:6). The scarlet reminds us of our redemption "in Christ Jesus, through faith in his blood" (Rom. 3:24, 25). The white is indicative of that life of purity which must characterize God's people. The cherubim reveal the fact that Christians are blessed by the ministry of angels (Heb. 1:14).

The white goat's hair curtain tells us that the church is a cleansed institution which is to remain clean (Eph. 5:26, 27).

The red rams' skins covering, made it is thought from the skins of the burnt offering (cp. Lev. 1:10), was a type of Christ crucified, a fact to be constantly kept in mind by the church (1 Cor. 2:2).

The sealskin, or porpoise-skin, completed the outside beauty of the type. In Ezekiel 16:9-14 Jerusalem is described as "shod with sealskin" and dressed in costly attire in order to make her "exceeding beautiful." The eternal glory of the new Jerusalem, the heavenly state of the church, is spoken of as that of "a bride adorned for her husband" (Rev. 21:2).

3) The Holy Place.—This was a type of the church where Christ is worshiped. The position of the type shows that it referred to things beyond the outer court where in type one becomes a Christian. Paul speaks of the Holy Place as "the first tabernacle" into which none but the priests were allowed to enter (Heb. 9:6, cp. 2). Since all in the church are priests (1 Pet. 2:9), it is certain that the first room in the tent was typical of the church and its services of Christian worship.

(a) Door, Exodus 26:36, 37.—It consisted of a veil of fine linen embroidered in blue, purple, and scarlet, and hung on five golden pillars set in sockets of brass.

As a type the door has to do with the new birth which is the entrance into the Kingdom of God, the church (John 3:3). As prerequisites for passing through the door attentions were given to the altar and the laver. The meaning of the whole journey from the altar into the tabernacle is given in the New Testament. Christ, our altar, is preached, men hear and believe the message, repent of their sins, confess him before men, and are immersed into his name (cp. Acts 2:14, 37, 38; Rom. 10:9). These matters attended to admit people into the church of Christ. The five pillars on which the veil was hung suggest the four Gospels and the Book of Acts, for the information in those books is necessary to make one a Christian. The facts in the first four enable him to believe in

Christ; the Book of Acts tell him how to be saved from his past sins.

(*b*) Furniture.—Having entered the first room of the tent, three objects meet our eyes.

(1) Table of showbread, Exodus 25:23-30.—This article, which stood on the north side (Exod. 40:22), was 2 cubits long, 1 cubit wide, 1½ cubits high, made of acacia wood overlaid with gold. It was carried by means of gold covered staves, one on each side. Its dishes, spoons, flagons, and bowls were of pure gold. Every sabbath there were placed upon it twelve cakes, six in a row, and incense was put on each row (Lev. 24:5-9). The bread was called showbread (Heb. Presence-bread), because it stood before Jehovah. The old loaves were eaten by the priests and the incense was burned unto Jehovah.

The teaching of the type is understood in the New Institution. As in the tabernacle so in the church there is the Table of the Lord. In each case certain important matters appear.

First, the time.—By divine appointment the typical table was set each week on the sabbath day. For the same reason the Lord's Table is set in the church every week on the first day (Acts 20:7). Had this been observed by the followers of Christ, the different churches would not now set the Lord's Table monthly, or quarterly, or semiannually, or annually. Such practice is in opposition to the divine arrangement.

Second, the loaves.—The twelve cakes, one for each tribe, represented the whole of Israel. In like manner the one loaf on the Lord's Table represents the whole church. Paul says, "We, who are many, are one bread, one body" (1 Cor. 10:17). By the fact of the one bread he argues for the unity of Christ's people. A divided church is contrary to the teaching of the Lord's Supper. Moreover, the typical bread was "for a memorial" of nourishment divinely given the children of Israel in their wilderness journey. The like purpose of the Lord's Supper Jesus designated in the words, "This do in remembrance of me" (Luke 22:19, 20). The emblems of his broken body and shed blood direct the mind to him who is our spiritual nourishment while in the earthly pilgrimage (John 6:35). Those who habitually absent themselves from his table will become weak, sickly and finally spiritually dead (cp. 1 Cor. 11:30). Furthermore, the fact that the loaves were eaten by the priests exclusively signifies that the Lord's Table is for the Lord's people only, all of whom constitute the "royal priesthood."

Third, the incense.—It was placed upon the loaves and then burned unto Jehovah. The significance of this was revealed by the Savior himself when he instituted his supper. Because the incense was a type of prayer, he "blessed" the bread and "gave thanks" for the cup (Matt. 26:26, 27). On this account his followers, when they gather at his table, offer to God the incense of thanksgiving for the loaf and cup.

(2) The lampstand, Exodus 25:31-39.—This beautiful light stood on the left, or south side (Exod. 40:24). It and its utensils were made of a talent of pure gold, in the value about $35,000 (Exod. 37:24). In form it had a central stem with three branches on each side, and seven lamps. The ornaments consisted of cups like almond blossoms, knops and flowers. The lamps were fed with pure olive oil and burned continually (Exod. 27:20). It was the only light for this room.

Concerning the typical meaning of the lampstand we are left in no doubt. It was a type of the word of God (Ps. 119:105), and as such it teaches some very important truths.

First, the light for God's house.—As it was the only light for the Holy Place, so the word of God is the only light for the church. For that reason the early Christians unremittingly attended to "the apostles' teaching," and no other (Acts 2:42). By that they were to "grow in grace and knowledge unto salvation" (2 Pet. 3:18; 1 Pet. 2:2). It settled all their church problems, as is revealed in the apostolic letters to the churches. Even their preaching was limited by that word (2 Tim. 4:2; 1 Pet. 4:11).

Second, the perfection of this light.—There were seven lamps, a number of perfection, completeness. Such is one characteristic of God's revelation. It is "perfect," hence by it the man of God is "furnished completely unto every good work" (Ps. 19:7; 2 Tim. 3:16, 17).

Third, the supply for this light.—The lamps were fed with pure olive oil, a type of the Holy Spirit who gave God's revelation to the church (1 Cor. 2:9, 10, 13).

Fourth, the constancy of the light.—The lamps should "burn continually," which suggests the eternity of God's word (Ps. 119:89) and also the activity of the church. As the priests were commissioned to keep the lamps burning continually, so Christians are forever to "hold forth the word of life" (Phil. 2:16). The church is "the pillar and ground of the truth" (1 Tim. 3:15).

(3) The altar of incense, Exodus 30:1-10.—This piece of furniture stood before the veil to the Most Holy Place. In construction it was 1 cubit square, 2 cubits high, made of acacia wood covered with gold. The top had a horn on each corner, an ornamental crown of gold, and below the crown at two of the corners were two gold rings for the staves by which it was carried. Every morning and evening highly perfumed incense was burned upon it with fire from the brazen altar. The sweet fragrance filled the room and penetrated the veil into the Most Holy.

In both the Old and New Testaments incense is spoken of as the type of prayer (Ps. 141:2;

Rev. 5:8). The altar of incense presents some very definite teaching concerning prayer.

First, in its position.—It stood just before the veil and is spoken of as "before the throne" (Rev. 8:3), because it was directly before the veil to the throne room. That is why in prayer we are said to "draw near unto the throne of grace" (Heb. 4:16). Our altar of incense is therefore the only place on earth where we get nearest God.

Second, in its connection with the altar of burnt offerings.—Fire for burning the incense was taken from that altar (Lev. 16:12), any other was spoken of as "strange fire" (Lev. 10:1) and was rejected by Jehovah. On the Day of Atonement blood of the sin offering, shed at the brazen altar, was applied to the altar of incense (Lev. 16:18, 19). Manifestly the teaching is this: The sacrifice of our Lord, typified by the altar of burnt offering, makes it possible for men to pray and be heard.

Third, in the composition of its incense.—Upon this altar there must be neither "strange fire" nor "strange incense." The various spices to be used were named by Jehovah and compounded "after the art of the perfumer" (Exod. 30:9, 34-38). In harmony with the type we find divine requirements for acceptable prayer. They are; faith in Christ (Jas. 1:6), according to God's revealed will (1 John 5:14), in a forgiving spirit (Matt. 6:12-15), and in the name of Christ (Col. 3:17). Jesus made prayer a condition on which we receive from God (Matt. 7:7, 8).

Fourth, in its service.—The offering of incense was "perpetual." Morning and evening its fragrance permeated the sanctuary. In comparison with this Christians are exhorted to "pray without ceasing." One characteristic of the early church was that her people "continued stedfastly in the prayers" (1 Thess. 5:17; Acts 2:42). Furthermore, only washed priests were permitted to come to the altar of incense. The teaching is that only baptized believers have the privilege of prayer. According to the type prayer is located in the church, but in modern teaching and practice the divine arrangement has been changed. The altar of incense has been carried out of the Holy Place, the church, into the court, the world, and there placed beyond the altar of sacrifice. The sinner, in becoming a Christian, is instructed first to pray.

4) The Most Holy Place.—This room was a type of heaven where Christ is seen. Such is the meaning given it by inspiration. Paul, in his exposition of the tabernacle, tells us that as the Jewish high priest entered into "the second" tabernacle once a year with atonement blood, so Christ "through his own blood entered into heaven itself, now to appear before the face of God for us" (Heb. 9:7, 11, 12, 24). In John's vision of heaven he saw the great blood-washed multitude and "the Lamb that is in the midst of the throne" being their shepherd (Rev. 7:13-17). Like the type, the new Jerusalem "lieth foursquare: the

length and the breadth and the height thereof are equal" (Rev. 21:16).

(*a*) The veil, Exodus 26:31, 32.—This division between the rooms reached from wall to wall and is spoken of as "the second veil" (Heb. 9:3). In texture, colors, and embroidery it was like the first, with one difference, it had figures of cherubim. This beautiful curtain was hung on four golden pillars set in sockets of silver.

As the way into the Holy Place, the veil was typical of the sacrificed body of Christ, called "a new and living way" by which we enter the heavenly holy place (Heb. 10:19, 20). Before the Savior's death the way to heaven was closed, a fact proclaimed by the typical veil (Heb. 9:8), but when he expired on the cross, "the veil of the temple was rent in two from top to bottom" (Matt. 27:51). This act of God signified that the way to heaven was opened by the death of his Son. The four pillars on which the veil was suspended might have been typical of the four divisions of the New Testament—the Gospels, Acts, Epistles, and Revelation—for all are needed in order to obtain "entrance into the eternal kingdom."

(*b*) The ark, Exodus 25:10-22.—At length we have reached the audience chamber of the King where he spoke to his people. Within was but one piece of furniture, a chest 2½ cubits long, 1½ cubits broad and 1½ cubits high, made of acacia wood and overlaid with gold inside and out.

Around the top it had an ornamental crown of gold. Its legs had four rings in which staves were fastened for transportation. For a cover it had a slab of pure gold called "the mercy-seat," on top of which were two golden cherubim facing each other with outspread wings. Within the ark was "a golden pot holding the manna, and Aaron's rod that budded, and the tables of the covenant" (Heb. 9:4). The only light for this room was the glory of Jehovah.

The spiritual significance of the ark is seen in its design. The fact that it contained divine law, or government, and was the place of Deity's manifestation, leads to the conclusion that it was intended as a type of the throne of God. This meaning is in harmony with the room itself which was a miniature heaven on earth. It is also established by John's vision at heaven's door, for he saw "a throne set in heaven, and one sitting upon it" (Rev. 4:2).

The revelation contained in the details of the ark is of absorbing interest.

The cherubim represented the heavenly messengers who are interested in and employed with reference to man's salvation (1 Pet. 1:12). Isaiah saw them (6:1-3), and so did John (Rev. 5:11).

The mercy-seat was a type of Christ. The Hebrew term for mercy-seat, *kapporeth,* is equal to the Greek word, *hilasterion,* rendered "propitiation" in 1 John 2:2; 4:10, and means a covering; hence Jesus is called the covering for our sins.

And as the mercy-seat was sprinkled with blood on the Day of Atonement (Lev. 16:14, 15), so Christ is our "propitiation (covering) through faith in his blood" (Rom. 3:25).

The arrangement of the type is revealing. Within the ark were "the tables of the testimony" witnessing against man, because he had broken the law of Jehovah. But the mercy-seat was between the law and the sinner, which signified that divine mercy intervenes between the two. Therefore, Paul could say of God, in speaking of his kindness, that "according to his mercy he saved us" (Titus 3:4, 5).

The articles in the ark carried their lessons. The tables of the covenant within, with the Book of the Law by the side (Deut. 31:26), indicated that the throne of God is the seat of revelation and final authority in religion. The pot of manna was a memorial of divine supply of bread for Israel in their journey from Egypt to Canaan (Exod. 16:33, 34), and it points to the fact that Jehovah is the material and spiritual support of his people. Aaron's rod that budded (See Num. 16, 17) symbolized divinely appointed leadership among Jehovah's people. The lesson is that in the official ministry of revealed religion "no man taketh the honor unto himself" (Heb. 5:4). As Jehovah designated the ministry in the type, so his Son has named the offices and made known the personal qualifications of his servants in the church.

The Jewish tabernacle presents a pictorial summary of man's journey from earth to heaven. In the outer court, or the world, he is seen as a sinner "having no hope and without God." Here the Redeemer is preached, believed, and obeyed, and the man far from God is "made nigh in the blood of Christ." In the first room of the tent, typical of the church, the sinner's condition is changed. He has "passed out of death into life." He is no longer an alien, but a member "of the household of God" where he may sit at the divine table, have access to the throne of grace, and live in the light of God's Word. The second room of the sanctuary, the throne room of the King and a picture of heaven, is a prophecy of man's eternal destiny. Since this Most Holy Place was entered through the first apartment, the arrangement was meant to signifiy that the way to heaven is through the church of Christ. Moreover, from this room issue mercy, angelic ministry, and divine revelation—all of which are needed in order to enter the Father's house.

CONCLUSIONS

In this course of study we have seen how God has instructed mankind by prophetic pictures.

There is a marked variety. *Persons,* such as Adam, Abraham, Moses, and others have by character and conduct been made to speak of the day of Christ. *Things,* like the altar, the laver, the tent, and its furniture were used to represent the coming Savior and how he brings people to the heavenly glory. *Institutions,* in the nature of sacrifices and holy festivals have shown that in sin is death and that man should give time and thought to matters of eternal consequence. *Offices,* occupied by prophet, priest, and king have been employed to teach that man needs instruction, forgiveness, and government. *Events,* like the flood, the passing through the Red Sea, the wilderness journey, the crossing of the Jordan, teach how the sinner is delivered and what his subsequent experience is to be. Thus by manifold teaching and constant repetition God has aroused and sustained interest in the learner who is disposed to study the "things that accompany salvation."

There is also comprehensive subject matter. The heinousness of sin is impressively set forth in unclean animals, in leprosy, and in divers washings. On the other hand, there is the beauty of holiness indicated by the clean animals, manifested by the white garments of the priests, and elaborated in the exquisite tabernacle and its services. Redemption through shed blood, the recovery of life lost by life given, is the doctrine of absorbing interest in all sacrifices. Finally, man's fellowship with God here and hereafter, mediated by His Son, is the great objective in this wonderful system of divine education. What, then, is the destiny of man redeemed? That is the desideratum read on every page of sacred history. The answer is found in the glorified man, Christ Jesus: "We shall be like him; for we shall see him even as he is."

www.ingramcontent.com/pod-product-compliance
Lightning Source LLC
Chambersburg PA
CBHW050758160426
43192CB00010B/1564